DEALS ON WHEELS

by
Gordon Page

A FIRESIDE BOOK
Published by Simon & Schuster, Inc.
NEW YORK

I dedicate this book to my patient and understanding wife, Linda; our three great sons, Gordon Jr., Lance, and Todd; our mothers, Bertha Page and Hedy Stenzel; and my departed father, Edward Page, who built and sold automobiles for 36 years. Also to William Woodin, Evelyn Poling, John Wink, Roy Rasmussen, and Bob Hunter—the best employees a dealer could have—as well as to the memories of three departed friends.

A Fireside Book

Published by Simon & Schuster, Inc.
Simon & Schuster Building
Rockefeller Center
1230 Avenue of the Americas
New York, New York 10020

FIRESIDE and colophon are registered trademarks of Simon & Schuster, Inc.

Designed by Stanley S. Drate/Folio Graphics

Manufactured in the United States of America

10 9 8 7 6 5 4 3

Library of Congress Cataloging in Publication Data

Page, Gordon.
    Deals on wheels.

    "A Fireside book."
    1. Automobiles—Purchasing. I. Title.
TL162.P327   1985   629.2'222'029   85-2095
ISBN: 0-671-55430-1

Acknowledgments

I wish to thank Dr. Norman Dohn, journalism professor at Ohio University, for key suggestions at the beginning; *Milwaukee Journal* editor Dick Leonard, for continuous help from the beginning of this writing project; Wade H. Mosby, author and former staff editor for the *Journal*, for his key suggestions; Jack Matthews, author and English professor at Ohio University, and Jill Briscoe, author, for their advice; and Barbara Marinacci for her editing.

Executive consultants Richard Allen Winter and Dr. Whitt Schultz offered vital encouragement and advice. So did literary agent Larry Sternig, Bob Pradt of Pine Mountain Press, Bill Woodin, Bob Cook, Chuck Green, Mac Norris, Jim McDonald, Don Peterson, Lee Iacocca, Bill Stevens, and Fred Stratton.

For their contributions to the text, I thank General Motors Corporation, Chrysler Corporation, Ford Motor Co., American Motors Corporation, BMW, Honda, Isuzu, Jaguar Cars, Mazda, Mercedes-Benz, Mitsubishi, Nissan Motor Corporation, Peugeot, Porsche, Renault, Rolls Royce, Subaru, Toyota, Volkswagen, Volvo, Briggs and Stratton, Excalibur Motor Company, the Edison Museum, and Bob Lienert of *Automotive News*.

For their input, I thank Milt Taylor, the late Paul Doucas, Bob Schlytter, Len Immke, Jake Sutherlin, Bobby Butts, Jim Love, Norm Wiese, Norman Braman, Jim Tracy, Wally Rank, Les Vogel, George Riggs, Michael Clauder, Paul Singer, John Rozatti, John Staluppi, Bob Maione, Don Lia, Alan Richards, Steve Hull, Clint Fowlkes, Jr., Fred Klipsch, Steve Barnett, Marv Tamaroff, Norm Merollis, Bill Deffebach, Fred Schneider, Tom Benson, Tony Frascona, Bob Schlossman, Irv Pentler, Buddy Braun, Ray Morris, Jack Safro, Don Corlett, Bud Jellerson, Hank Candler, Fred Beans, Hal Lyons, Frank Holtham, Sam Angiuli, Ed Walmsley, Ed Trotta, Gary Fesler, George Morris, Art Mele, Gailen Smith, Gary Hancock, Charles Smith, Bill Templeton, Bill Wise, Bill Berger, Gus Schneider, John Golestani, Allen Holzhauer, John Chase, B. G. Read, Jimmy Carter, Roger Dean, the late Don McCullagh, Jack McCullagh, Carl Schneider, Dick Shalla, the late Don Haley, Ernie Rogers, Gary Fronrath, Don Lucas, Terry Yates, Brian Roundtree, Jim Blau, Reed Nodell, Bob Tolkan, Phil Tolkan, Jake Sweeny, Jerry Holz, Bud Selig, Woody Jebson, George Olson, Ray Durdin, Lou Bachrodt, Vic Potamkin, Jim Long, Bill Knafel, Kenny Ausman, Andy Hall, Mike Miller, Roger Kresge, Buck Riley, Roger Holler, Larry Balistreri, Dick Romero, Rudy Kraft, Bob Long, Rick Middlekauf, Cecil VanTyle, Lou McKernon, Cal Worthington, Ralph Williams, John Blessing, Rick Galles, Bobby Unser, A. J. Foyt, Doug Janisch, Bob Mitchell, Dan Drout, Craig Bernard, Phil Schilabra, Ted Gordon, Gordie Boucher, Jack Kelly, Bob Johnson, Dave Bouchet, Shirley Salcheck, and Tracy Johnson (from Able Polygraph). I appreciate the help of Rosann Lahr, Laura Lehman, Amy Mitchell, Shari Dobush, Carolee Ruhnke, and Carol Anderson.

Thanks to the following people for reading and criticizing the manuscript in various stages: William Woodin, former GM executive and employee; Richard Leonard of the *Milwaukee Journal;* Wade Mosby, former editor of the *Milwaukee Journal* Green Sheet; Harry Fritz, language consultant and writer; Supervisor of Milwaukee Public High Schools Emil Rucktenwald and his wife Marion; Price-Waterhouse partner Don Nicolaisen and his wife Sandy; Dave Funk and his wife Diane; B. Dalton manager Paul Wells; Jack Lackner of J. Lackner & Associates; Executive Vice President of Cross-Treucker Richard Lindgren and his wife Lois; WISN Public Affairs Director Don Froehlich; Bob Mitchell and Doug Janisch, project engineers for Briggs and Stratton; Jean Sollen; and attorneys William Glassner and Howard Tolkan. For their suggestions, I thank J. Patrick Wright, Joe Girard, Jane Jordan Browne, and Ray Peekner.

Thanks to all my wonderful employees and business friends, such as Bill Woodin, Evelyn Poling, John Wink, Roy Rasmussen, Bob Hunter. . .The list could go on and on, to include thousands of clients who have touched my life in the past 28 years, who purchased a car or truck, or had my firms perform service work for them.

Above all, I thank God for being my partner, for supplying daily guidance, particularly during the writing of this book, and for bringing the right people into my life at the right time.

Gordon Page is available as a speaker—he is always interested in hearing from his readers and may be reached by writing or calling: Gordon Page, P.O. Box 432, Brookfield, WI 53005, 414/781-1846.

Contents

To the Reader

Americans will buy more than twenty-five million automobiles this year, nine million new and sixteen million used. First-time buyers will account for at least a million of these sales. It's a sad fact that lack of experience will cost them cash. Even many repeat buyers still haven't learned the basics of purchasing and selling cars.

At the other end of the spectrum, we have a few unethical car salesmen and dealers, people who will use every trick in the trade to separate extra cash from customers.

This book will furnish buyers with inside information about the automobile industry by showing what goes on behind the scenes of a car sales and service business. Paradoxically, it will also serve the car salesman or dealer by forcing the few bad apples of the industry to clean up their acts and become professionals. One dealer told me that every business has at least ten percent bad in it—and that the car business has fifteen percent. Another, less critical, dealer told me every business is five percent bad, and the car business is no exception.

People don't realize that they're not so much *buying* a car as *spending* their hard-earned money—and that applies to everything. To net $100, people earn $130 pretax, plus blood, sweat, and tears. Doesn't it make sense to spend a little energy making a car deal and keep some of that hard-earned money? Give yourself a raise, America!

Every buyer must know exactly what he or she wants. A plan is essential. If you don't know what you want, the odds are that you won't get it. Why buyers would wander into an auto dealership prepared to spend anywhere from $5,000 to $50,000 without knowing exactly what they want is mind-boggling. Yet they do it thousands of times daily.

This book will show you how to decide exactly what you want. Also, you will learn how to research your dream auto. Armed with information about car models, competitive pricing, options, and dealer strengths and weaknesses, you will be prepared to handle the most important facet of car buying—negotiating. You'll learn how to negotiate in the four areas that determine the overall investment in your car: interest rate, insurance rate, price and trade-in value.

In ancient marketplaces, buyers tried to buy as low as they could and sellers tried to sell as high as they could. The haggling was simply to settle on a price that seemed fair to both parties. More than two thousand years ago, Ahab the camel seller said: "I want two hundred drachmas for my camel." And David the shrewd camel buyer responded, "Oy, I'll give you twenty." Somewhere between the asking price and the offer they eventually agreed. And afterward Ahab said, "That's the most anybody ever got for a two-humped camel like that." And David thought to himself, "No one has ever bought a two-humped camel this cheap before." So Ahab went away thinking he had bested David, while David was thinking he had really skinned Ahab.

This same bargaining has carried over into the car-buying process. Yet North American buyers don't like to negotiate, and they pay dearly for their reluctance. Because of a distaste for haggling, the buyer lets the seller set the price.

Unfortunately, most Americans have the department-store shopper's habit of paying whatever price is printed on the tag. Continuing this practice in the car dealership will cost you hundreds—maybe thousands—of dollars. If you approach buying with more knowledge, self-confidence, and assertiveness, the outcome will favor your savings account.

My original goal in writing this book was to make you a "professional buyer." But another purpose emerged. As I began to explain the psychology and realities of salesmanship to buyers, I realized that many car professionals could use tips on improving their effectiveness in the marketplace. Besides converting prospects into satisfied customers, they must make consistent, continuing efforts to provide courteous and quality service after the sale.

Then there is the strange tension connected with buying a car. As one auto executive told me:

> I've always been bothered that there is so much fear about car buying on both the salesman's and the customer's part. I think basically it's because of two things: (1) a car is a large investment item; and (2) there have never been stable, fixed prices for cars.
> Then there are two other points to ponder. Salesmen have never sold

on the basis that a car is an investment, like a house. Yet an equity investment is real! Furthermore, this is the only business in which a trade-in is usually involved. *Herein lies a basic problem in reaching an agreement.* The customer not only has a lack of understanding of how a car depreciates, but a personal feeling of worth of *his* car. This causes the transaction to become other than an economic purchase such as stocks and bonds.

Then, all too often a customer contacts a salesman who simply does not have the authority to accept a deal without conferring with a manager or dealer, whom the customer rarely meets. This uncertainty undermines the customer's confidence in the selling situation itself. "Why can't I simply find out the cost to *me?*" he or she wonders.

Somehow we must remove all the hocus pocus from the transaction of car buying.

I have tried to supply information about these issues and many others involved with car buying.

Certainly, my book may cause some raised eyebrows. A few will wonder, "Did he have to say that?. . .Now everyone knows our trade secrets!"

After my self-published edition started appearing in Milwaukee bookstores at the end of 1983, a Milwaukee dealer asked me, "How could you write a book like this, since you were one of us?"

I asked him, "Did you read it?"

"No, I'd probably have a heart attack if I did," he said.

This book was not intended to be an exposé. However, it does tell about merchandising automobiles in a frank, no-holds-barred style by someone who has spent twenty-five years inside the business. I believe the purchase of an automobile should be a "win-win" proposition instead of one where someone loses. When the buyer and seller begin to regularly strike mutually satisfactory bargains, the whole industry will prosper.

So I ask all my friends and clients in the auto industry to understand that one day someone was going to write a book like this. It is best that it was written by someone who actually understands the entire automotive business through long experience within it.

If it appears to you that this book is critical of the retail auto industry, ask yourself, "How much longer can the industry be pounded as it has been?" By bringing all the so-called mysteries, secrets, and suspicions into the open and clearing them up, this book will help to strengthen the survivors.

I have had many apprehensions in publishing this revelatory book and actually delayed until my friends convinced me that I should proceed. I am doing so because I believe that an informed public will only strengthen the present and future of our great automotive industry, and thereby our nation. We cannot change the past. But if we do not learn from the past, we are doomed to repeat it.

Soaking up so much useful, hard information can be hard work, so I've tried to give your eyes and mind welcome relief by having talented Milwaukee artist Luis Machare provide amusing cartoons depicting the jungle atmosphere that often pervades the auto showroom.

A note about language usage: lest I offend the female gender, please bear in mind that the generic terms "he" and "salesman" were used for my own convenience in writing and do not refer to a particular sex.

Truly, I hope the next time we meet, you will be traveling on a new set of wheels.

The Tale of Timid Tilly

Houston's Timid Tilly wanted to buy a new car. Having bought three cars previously, she had learned all too late that she could have: (1) purchased each of them for considerably less money; (2) received more money for her trade-in cars; and (3) gotten a lower interest rate.

Tilly had always had a hard time expressing herself, and would blurt out things that she really did not intend to say. Also, when she was tense she tended to forget important things. She became especially nervous and shy whenever she entered that arena of the car pro—an automobile showroom. And she recalled how submissive she had been in the past when confronted by salesman Ace Silvertone. She would end up buying the car he wanted her to buy, at the price he set for it.

But this time Tilly—who was a very organized and disciplined person—constructed a plan. Someone who knew a lot about selling techniques had told her, "The person who breaks the silence in a sales situation loses." She was going to be close-mouthed, hold her ground, and buy the car *she* wanted. At a lower cost, too, than he would like.

So what did Tilly do? She wrote out what she called "Seven Sets of Seven Magic Words" on 3″ × 5″ cards. At home she practiced saying them in sequence, again and again, until they sounded firm and natural to her. Then she went into the car showroom.

When Ace saw her, he came forward, smiling and rubbing his hands. But Tilly was no longer putty in his hands! After he saw that she meant business and that she could not be charmed by his sales pitch, he decided to propose a better deal than the ones he had made for her in the past. Tilly, telling him that she would consider it, left the astounded Ace and went off to talk with several other dealerships—still using her Seven Sets of Seven Magic Words. The salesmen there offered more attractive deals than Ace had. Tilly went back and told him so.

Ace wanted to keep Tilly as a customer but also needed to make a sale that day. He came up with the best deal yet. And Tilly—who really did like Ace—signed the contract soon afterward.

She had saved herself hundreds of dollars by sticking to her plan.

A car-buying plan is very important, and the next few chapters will tell you how to make your own. And if *you* want to know the secret of Tilly's Seven Sets of Seven Magic Words—what they are and why they work so well—read on. (You'll find them in Chapter 8.)

I feel like a tiger with these flash-cards!!!

ONE

Before You Shop for a Car

Melvin and Edna, wide-eyed and smiling, walked into Boonesburg's largest car dealership and were welcomed by Peter Vasalino (one of the boys from the big city). Melvin was treated to a "how-you-been-ole-buddy" pat on the back, while Edna received an ear-to-ear smile.

"We've come to trade cars," Edna announced. "We brought a pig, a cow, and two thousand dollars in savings," she added proudly. "We want to buy a new Wild Fire. We just love it!" Grinning, Melvin wordlessly agreed, bobbing his head up and down.

Peter's words flowed like honey. "Just sign right here. . .and you'll drive home in the car of your dreams."

After signing the contract, Melvin squeezed Edna's hand. They beamed at one another, each knowing that this purchase was going to bring sudden glamour into their lives.

Sharp, car-savvy Peter took possession of their old car, livestock, and cash, and made arrangements to finance the balance. He had sold them a new car—sight unseen.

Melvin and Edna were innocents who had wandered into the car-buying jungle. And they weren't aware that they had been taken. Eagerness and enthusiasm had clouded their judgment. They didn't learn the total price of the car, the rate of interest they would be paying for financing, what their payments would be and for how long. They were also ignorant of the amount of allowance granted on their old car, whether their new auto had two or four doors, or what sort of options their dream machine had—including engine and transmission.

Hard to imagine such a thing could happen? Believe me, this story is not as farfetched as it might seem. Naive and enthusiastic people tend to get carried away in an auto showroom, forgetting all common sense. They'll pay sticker price (a manufacturer's suggested list price), or even higher, to get what they *think* they want. They won't examine or question what is being sold for what price. This shortsightedness inevitably results in excess profits for the seller.

Melvin and Edna were "L.D.'s" (lay-downs or easy marks in car biz jargon) who may have spent an extra $5,000. Most car buyers would not make all of the mistakes this couple made. However, if you have lost out in car dealing before, odds are you will repeat your mistakes.

Fewer than half of all buyers ever try to negotiate with car sellers. They continue to miss out on potential savings of hundreds or thousands of dollars. Why? Because they are afraid. People who are customarily assertive will suddenly turn shy and uncertain when shopping for a car. The ones who bargain do so timidly, embarrassed to haggle over prices. To make matters worse, they will pay for this timidity twice, the second time being when they change roles with the dealer and sell their used car for less than it is worth.

The real question is, how can you avoid all of these amateur mistakes and pitfalls when dealing with professionals? There's only one way: preparation.

Cutting through Confusions

It's easy to understand why today's car buyer is baffled. Not only have prices skyrocketed, but interest rates can be higher than those charged by loan sharks a few short years ago. Add to this literally hundreds of car models, colors, electronics, engines, and thousands of advertising claims. It's a wonder a decision is ever reached. Yet you must decide on what you want *before* going in to bargain with the seller.

"How," you may ask, "can I make a decision before I go in to a dealership?"

Here's an easy way.

Dream Research

Let your imagination run wild! Look at magazine ads and at real cars themselves out on the street or through the large dealership windows. (Be cautious—don't stray inside until you are absolutely ready.)

At this point, money is no object. You are just shopping in your mind, doing dream research. Look at the good features and criticize the shortcomings. Look at the wide range of colors. The greater the variety of cars you see, the better. Remember, you are playing the field, and there are no strings attached. It should be fun.

You will come up with a long list of models, colors, and options that you like.

Establish Priorities

Now that you have your wish list it's time to roll up your shirtsleeves and get down to work.

Gather the people who will figure in your final decision and, together, rate each of the features on your list. Put a "1" by each *must item*. For example, if the car is to be used for family transportation it must have the required passenger capacity. Features that are not quite so important would receive a "2," etc.

The important thing is that your list be rated according to what the people involved need. Ask questions and solicit answers. Make everyone a part of the project. If you are deciding by yourself, try to find a friend or acquaintance who will play devil's advocate for an afternoon and question your reasoning on where you've placed certain items on your list.

Honesty is critical regardless of the size of the decision committee.

The beauty of listing by priority is that you can make decisions

without fear of making mistakes due to time pressures. You will
see—on paper—what is important to you and those involved. Later,
when a dealer offers you a super deal on an option you've previously
rated "6" or "7," you won't have to stop and think about it.

Develop a Plan

Nothing great was ever accomplished without a plan. Remember
Melvin and Edna? As bad as their deal was, at least they had a plan.
1. Buy a Wild Fire.
2. Take car, cash, pig, and cow for down payment.
3. Go to the dealership in Boonesburg.
4. Make a trade.
5. Drive Wild Fire home.
Get a sheet of paper and simply list the steps you must take.
Then go one step further. List the obvious obstacles you think you
will encounter. Ask yourself the following questions:
• What must I do to overcome the obstacles?
• What else must I know about the car I want?
• What must I know about financing?
• When is the best time to buy my new car?
• How do I figure the price I should pay?
• What is my old car worth?
• What must I know about car dealers?
• What must I know about car salesmen?
• How do I negotiate effectively?
You will have many unanswered questions—questions you must
be able to handle comfortably before you venture into a dealership.
The remainder of this book will either give you direct answers or
show you how and where to obtain them.

TWO

Timing Your Purchase

Sol and Sarah Workhard had checked car prices all over the Los Angeles area. Disappointed and exhausted, they concluded that it was impossible to buy a decent car at the price they had set.

But one day at lunch Sarah heard about a Wheeler-Dealer car store out in Compton. That evening, she and Sol cruised over to find out firsthand about the great deals that were supposedly available there.

Again, as he had so many times before, Sol handed the salesman his checklist, saying, "This is what we want in the way of car and equipment . . . and this is how much we can give. Do you have something for us?"

And much to his amazement, Buddy the Salesman, after looking over the list, told them: "You're a nice couple. Sure, we'll help you buy the car at *your* price. Just sign right here!"

Pleased though he was, Sol never signed anything without looking over what he was signing. So he now asked why the papers were dated October 3 instead of September 21—today's date.

Buddy's reply came quickly. "That's the date we will *deliver* the car to you. You see, October 3 is right after the new car showing. We receive a special bonus from the manufacturer at that time for selling any last-season cars. Because you're such a fine pair and you need a good discount to get the car you want, we're sharing the bonus with you."

The right *timing* was what saved Sol and Sarah money—though they hadn't known at all about this lucky possibility.

Plan Ahead for Your Buying

The best time to buy a car, truck, or van—any negotiable item, for that matter—is when you don't really *need* one.

When you buy a car quickly, either out of necessity or on the spur of the moment, you rarely make the wisest purchase. You haven't had time to work out a plan and set it into action. Nor can you wait for a time when some rebate program or other sales specials are offered.

This does not mean that you must plan months in advance, but it does mean that you shouldn't wait until your current car is on its very last wheel.

Timing is always an important element in buying a car. *Never* rush out and buy impulsively. On the other hand, don't procrastinate until you are so desperate for wheels that you'll have to take what is available.

Obviously there are situations in which you might need a car right away—after totaling one in an accident or landing a new job that requires more impressive transportation. Even then, though you may feel pressured, take time to make a plan—on paper!

Avoiding the Impulse to Buy

When you're considering a new car, you may be more susceptible than you think to showroom hoopla, special showings complete with balloons, music, and other attractions. Flush with excitement, you may buy a new car from sheer impulse. Even if you *are* ready to buy, don't throw caution to the winds.

Lest I sound like a killjoy, let me say that it's good to see what's going on, to join friends and neighbors in welcoming a new business or seeing the new models unveiled—or whatever (a "Jello Jump" is a terrific dealer gimmick for drawing hundreds of spectators). But stay cool and stick to your carefully devised plan.

I want to buy a car today!!!

Go ahead and sign up for the door prizes and take part in whatever other activities are being offered. Just be careful to stay in control when it comes to making a decision. Be aware that you've entered the territory of the pros—the professional salespeople. You must be prepared to become a pro yourself—a professional buyer—in order to match their skills with your own. Don't let anybody rush, intimidate, embarrass, or control you when you're buying a car. Look for a win/win situation. All it takes is a little preparation, nothing technical. With preparation you'll develop your own style of negotiating.

Their Supply and Your Demand

Nearly everyone nowadays understands the basic economic rule of supply and demand. When supply is plentiful and demand is low, the buyer's bargaining power is much stronger. But when supply is low and demand is high, the advantage shifts to the seller.

By choosing the right *time,* you can work this principle to your advantage. There are various important ingredients here: national economic conditions, regional economic conditions, seasonal changes, even days of the week, times of the day, and the weather.

Having the showroom to yourself is like money in the bank. If what follows seems troublesome to you, remember that taking the time to investigate when to buy a car could fatten your wallet by as much as $5,000!

Tough Economic Times Might Be a Good Time for You to Buy

We're all aware of the punishment that American car manufacturers have taken from foreign competitors. But they haven't abandoned operations yet, and let's hope they won't. Competition is healthy.

For a number of reasons which I'll discuss later in detail, domestic cars may be far better deals than imports. Because of diminished demand for their cars, American dealers are far more likely now to give ground to customers ready to buy.

Competition between sellers can work to your benefit, too. When the supply of new cars is high but demand does not meet it, dealers and the manufacturers behind them are anxious to move their merchandise into buyers' hands. In order to do so, they offer greater incentives—and better deals, perhaps—than their local competitors are giving. If the dealer in your town won't discuss a better price, consider going to the next town.

Staying in close touch with the national economic scene will help you decide what present and future tendencies make car buying more attractive.

Regional Economic Differences

The United States has not one economy but many. Some areas can be in a recession or a depression while others are booming.

Such southern states as gas-producing Louisiana and oil-producing Texas were affected less by the national recession of the early 1980s than the industrial North, where production was way down. High-technology areas on the East Coast—Boston, for example—fared better than Pittsburgh, Pa., and Lackawanna, N.Y., which were losing much of their steel industry.

Study these regional differences. You might consider buying a car downstate or across the state line where the economy is in worse shape. Someone else's misfortune could turn out to be your good fortune.

Seasonal Regional Differences

Seasonal differences are relatively obvious. Cars tend to sell better in good weather than in bad. In most parts of the country this makes for highs during the spring and lows for winter and summer.

But here again, the vast patchwork American geography and economy makes for some interesting phenomena. The Southwest has a very strong car market in August. Its drier heat is not as oppressive as the humid heat from which the rest of the nation suffers. The corn- and wheat-producing parts of the prairie states have a late fall harvest time, so that part of the country has a strong fall market. If the harvest is good, this region has a good fall car market. If it is not, the fall rally may not take place.

Two areas of the country have almost a "flat curve." Sales are fairly steady year-round in the New York City area and in southern Florida. The Big Apple seems to generate a consistent need for cars, no matter what the season or economy. Florida has good weather in its favor, as well as continuous growth, with the population doubling every ten to fifteen years. Even if fewer people end up buying cars, the fact that there are consistently more people coming in makes for an overall dependable market.

Although blessed with year-round good weather, California poses a special problem to car buyers: the heavy penetration of imports, which reduces the sale of American-made cars to approximately 55 percent statewide, with only 20 percent in some areas.

Other regional economic factors can affect car buying. For instance, bonuses issued to employees by a large corporation will put many potential buyers into the auto showrooms to compete with you—as happens, say, in Rochester, N.Y., when the 40,000 Kodak employees receive their annual bonuses.

When domestic new car showings begin in late September–early October, consumers are intensely interested in seeing and buying these brand-new models. But the manufacturers load up the large fleet companies at this time—National, Hertz, Avis, and the large leasing corporations—and the country's retail dealers are usually left short of the high-demand models. So be careful of buying a popular new car model at this time!

The Slowest Times of All

Even though people all over the country, without respect to region or weather or sometimes even sanity itself, are running all over and spending wildly during December and then paying for many of their purchases in January, the holiday season is usually the slowest time for a car dealer. People are preoccupied with holiday buying and celebrating. And holiday gifts generally are not as big or expensive as a car. Beware of telling a salesperson a car is a gift, and never indicate a deadline for buying, like Christmas Eve. Act as if time is not important. Otherwise, the price will be higher.

People who are not celebrating often find this season very gloomy indeed. So they are not inclined to buy cars either. Therefore, if you are in a position to shop for your car between December 20 and January 15, you will find dealers lonely and more than ready to bargain.

There are other slow weeks, such as the one in which federal income taxes are due, and the two just preceding and the one following it. People are busy filing their returns, hurting from having paid them, or in the doldrums for two weeks or so until their refund checks—if any—come in. Nationally, this makes for often the second slowest time of the year for car dealers. So if you are in a position to buy in April, take advantage of a time when dealers are hungry for your money!

Other slow times are weeks in which national holidays (Memorial Day, Fourth of July, Labor Day, Thanksgiving) occur. People are traveling and busy with big family celebrations, so they have no time to tend to the business of car buying.

Also, on the first two or three warm and sunny weekends after a long winter, people are inclined to get out of doors and work off cabin fever by doing yardwork and home maintenance or simply enjoying a drive through the countryside. The same thing can happen during the final beautiful weekends of autumn, before winter sets in.

And don't forget other special times that keep people from car showrooms: the opening of the hunting or fishing seasons, state and county fair weeks, popular festivals, or special sporting events to watch on television, such as the Olympics or the Super Bowl. And then there's Election Day, as well as the leadup to it.

Choosing the Best Day and Hour

Be sure to discover when the showrooms are the emptiest in your area, for those are the best times to get Deals on Wheels.

First, find out their hours. Some are open seven days a week, from early in the morning to late evening. Others are open on all weekdays and on certain evenings, on Saturday mornings but not at all on Sundays. You can usually check the salesroom hours in the phone company's Yellow Pages.

Watch for days in which business is slow—usually early in the week and before paydays. Pick the least busy day for doing your car shopping. In Milwaukee, for instance, consumers are used to most retail establishments vigorously advertising end-of-the-month sales. Many payrolls are doled out on the 15th and 30th of the month.

As for times of the day, weekday mornings are generally slow, especially early in the week. In blue-collar areas, crowds can come in between shift changes, while in white-collar areas showrooms are busiest when people leave work in the late afternoon or early evening. In farming areas, showrooms are empty when people are normally at home doing their chores. As a professional buyer you'll have to know the territory.

If you have discovered the slow times of the day and week in dealerships, it may be worth using a vacation day to do the major shopping for your car.

Consider the Weather

I have talked about climate and seasons in various regions of the country. Every place has some bad weather. This could mean snow in the North or intense heat in the South. Or vice versa—the unexpected extreme. Rainy days or plain old blah grayness might also keep people away.

You might think that people would go out shopping for cars in bad weather, since they can't work in their yards or engage in outdoor sports or go on picnics. But not so. Consequently, car salesmen get lonely and blue at such times.

So when you see a day that you, like everyone else, would prefer to spend by the fireside, napping, working on a hobby, or doing indoor chores, drop by a dealership and cheer up a salesman by proposing some deal that will decidedly favor you.

Be Alert to Dealers' Needs Too

If you shop during an economic low, in the right season, at the quietest hour of the slowest day in the slowest part of the month, you can improve your deal even more.

How? By being alert to an individual dealer's needs. Subtly ask the salesman how many cars have been sold during the day or week, and of those how many *he* has sold. More than likely he won't have prepared himself for your question and he'll tell you the unvarnished truth. If he replies with a low number or does not respond at all, ask how many cars he and the dealer normally sell in a day, week, month, or year. Be mindful of the salesman's or dealership's needs to get another car sold. They may be hungry and practically push one on you for whatever reasonable price you offer to pay.

Some dealers or sales managers have incentive bonus plans for the sales staff. They might offer bonuses to salesmen selling the first cars of each day or week, and perhaps a $50 to $500 bonus for lining up the highest gross profit deal or highest sales volume of the day, week, month, or year. Another favored incentive offered by manufacturers to both dealers and sales personnel is an all-expense-paid trip (but not tax-free!) to some exotic place. If you know of deals like these, get into the showroom and be some eager beaver's "first." He may be willing to make special concessions on price and features in order to sign you up.

Ask questions. Try to find out if your salesman is working on such an incentive basis and make it clear that you will be glad to help him win a Caribbean cruise.

When the end of a contest is near, you may be in a fortunate position indeed. Obviously, a salesman or sales manager might let a car go at very little profit if that sale would put him over the top in competing for a vacation in the South Seas.

As a result of such contests, my wife and I have taken sixteen trips to various parts of the world. We can certainly attest that salesmen, sales managers, and even dealership owners are all interested in winning. They regard these company-sponsored trips not only as a treat but also as a chance to exchange tips, compare notes, and generally enjoy a good time with others in the same business.

Waiting for the Model Year?

We used to hear a lot about people who were waiting for the new-car showing—that is, waiting for the new models to come out before they would buy. The once-customary fall new car unveilings, however, are customary no longer. Most U.S. companies have picked up a cue from foreign manufacturers and are showing a new model when it is ready for the public's eye rather than waiting.

Certainly you can consider buying just when the new models

come out. You'll enjoy the benefits of a new car longer and pay not much more—conceivably even less—for the privilege of being for a while the center of attention wherever you drive. Note, too, that a car introduced in the spring will remain a new car for a year and a half if the next new model is introduced in an autumn showing.

Still, models are going to change sometime for each car. You might well consider buying an outgoing model; usually these cars are more of a bargain because they are theoretically a year old when you buy them brand new.

Are the design changes between the model years matters of real concern to you? Are you attentive to the small engineering and design features here and there that are recognizable only by experts with manufacturers' manuals in hand? If not, what do you care if you don't get "the model year" as it first comes off the line? It doesn't change the mileage or the service you'll get out of the car. And unless you plan to trade it in very quickly, it won't affect the value nearly as much as proper care and feeding will.

Rebates on Last Year's Models

Some manufacturers give dealers an additional 5 percent year-end rebate on the old model, beginning on the day the new model comes out. Maybe a local dealer will share it with you. (Aha! Now you know a trade secret the average dealer won't share with you. But don't let him get away without mentioning this year-end rebate to *you*. If the salesman or dealer doesn't bring it up, you should do so. . .and show what a pro you are because you're aware of the tricks of their trade.)

Legally, from the manufacturer's point of view, the qualifying bonus or rebate cars are to be officially sold on or after the showing dates for new cars. Many dealers, however, disregard this rule—as Buddy the Salesman did when selling a car to Sarah and Sol Workhard in the story at the start of this chapter.

Many dealers have a few leftover models from the previous year which they use as advertising "leaders." Unless a car is a real "don't-wanter" (I'll talk about this more in Chapter 5), the dealers can actually make more profit selling a year-end rebate car than they would have if it were sold earlier, say in July, August, or September.

There are always the bargain hunters and sincere people who

claim they don't like the new models' styling or prices and therefore buy the leftovers. If you don't plan to trade every two or three years, the resale value of the year-older model won't be significantly lower than the newer model.

I can't tell you exactly when the model will change for every car. But a dealership can. This is another piece of timing information you should have before making your decision to buy.

But above all, keep time on *your* side in making a car deal.

We'll do it all for you and save you time.

THREE

How Will You Pay?

Philadelphia's Heidi and Herman Pennywise decided to buy a sleek new Moonbeam for $20,000 from Sleepy Sam. They told him they would pay cash. (Herman thought that if he did so, the dealer would sell for a lower price.) They put down a deposit of $500.

Herman went to Money Bucks, the neighborhood banker, and was told, "We aren't making auto loans at this time."

The Pennywises then went back to Sam and said that they had decided not to buy the Moonbeam. The salesman smiled and said, "Fine, we'll just charge you a five percent penalty—that's five hundred dollars plus your five-hundred-dollar deposit."

Herman and Heidi were horrified. They scurried off to their attorney, who told them that state law was on the dealer's side. It was intended to protect dealerships from people who were not fully intent on buying a car and who would waste their time and effort.

The Pennywises went back to Sleepy Sam. Throwing themselves on his mercy, they confessed that they really didn't have the cash after all, that they were going to get a bank loan but had been denied one.

Sam was a nice fellow. He didn't want to see anyone suffer. And he also preferred to sell a whole car to somebody rather than take money for nothing sold.

"No problem here," he reassured the Pennywises. "We'll finance your car for you. Actually we prefer to finance deals because the dealership makes money by handling financing arrangements and also selling various kinds of insurance."

And he used their $500 as part of the down payment.

Because financing is an important factor in selecting your new car, it should be investigated as part of your initial car-buying plan.

If you're not in a position to pay cash for the car you want, you've got a lot of company. About 95 percent of the car buyers in this country obtain financing through a variety of means.

Ask yourself a few vital questions when you start thinking about buying another car:

- Do you have enough cash to pay for your car in full? And even if you do, would it be wise to pay the whole price outright?
- What is the prevailing rate of interest? (Make sure you don't pay more; you can try to pay less.)
- What percent of the total price will a lender be willing to finance?
- Is your credit rating good enough to qualify for financing?
- How big a down payment can you make? If you have a specific car in mind, what is the minimum down payment on it?
- How much can you afford for monthly payments?
- How long do you expect to make monthly payments—12, 18, 24, 30, 36, 42, 48. . .or 60 months?

Should You Pay Cash or Finance?

Even if you have sufficient cash to purchase a new car outright, you might well ponder whether you wish to pay more than just a substantial down payment on a car. (Used cars aren't so difficult to finance, of course, especially if they're old.)

An emergency might require some quick money, and if you've exhausted a lot of it on the car, you may have some difficult scrambling to do—selling stocks and bonds, for instance, that you'd prefer to hold on to as investments. You might even have to sell the car itself, which consumed most of your savings, at a disappointing price.

Consider, too, that you might be able to put a large chunk of your cash to work for you at a higher rate of interest than you would be paying on a car loan. And you could even pay off the loan early if you watch your money closely.

Also keep in mind that many states have "lemon laws" that protect you when you buy a car. Under some laws, if your new car has a problem that isn't repaired after three visits to a dealership service department—within a thirty-day period—you can have a new one, or a refund. You must attempt to have it repaired during the first year of factory warranty. Under other laws, if you have financed your car and have a problem with it that cannot be repaired to your reasonable satisfaction, you can stop payments until it is repaired. (Make certain that your local laws do indeed protect you in case you are forced to stop payment.)

The Dealer's Part in Financing Transactions

Although it's widely believed that dealers will give you a better deal when you pay cash for a new car, it turns out this isn't always so.

Today more and more dealerships are in the car insuring and financing business as sideline ventures. They should be open to granting concessions in a deal they would finance *if* you let them know you're aware they'll profit from bankrolling your purchase. So make this situation work to your advantage in lowering the price or gaining options.

Most dealers prefer a customer's finance deal to involve credit life, accident, and health insurance. Credit life insurance adds a small premium to your payment but pays off the balance owed on your car in the event of your death. This protects both the lender and your family, which could keep the car without making further payments.

Accident and health insurance is similar, in that it keeps your car payments up in the event of an accident or illness that keeps you from working. Check on the qualifications in each individual policy. Most do not pay on preexisting conditions (in other words, if you sign a finance contract with credit life and/or health/accident insurance after having been diagnosed as seriously ill and then *that* illness prevents you from working, the policy will not pay). Most impose waiting periods of six, twelve, or twenty-one days *after* you are out of work before the policy begins making payments.

Dealers are interested in your own financial protection because often they have a stake in it themselves. Some dealers must sign a recourse or repurchase contract with the lender. Others have the option to do so. Different areas of the country have different requirements. The policy is generally decided by the financial institution handling the loan.

The dealer who signs a recourse or repurchase contract is exposing his dealership to a greater risk than the dealer who isn't bound by such an agreement. This means that if for some reason the buyer defaults on his loan and the financial institution has to take the car back, the dealership is liable to the finance company. It's my opinion that this is not a good way to do business. The financial institution has the best of both worlds with little liability, whereas the dealer often bears the brunt of handling the physical repossession—and then of having to fix up and resell the car.

If a dealer has a finance company as a sideline venture, and has the money and will to run it well, more power to him! The dealer then becomes the banker too, and there is a certain convenience, as well as additional profit, in this arrangement. In some cases the tie-in can work to the customer's advantage.

Mechanical breakdown insurance (extended warranty) is offered by most dealers at extra cost. If you think you need it, buy it. An expensive repair may occur at a financially inconvenient time.

Serious problems in new cars generally occur in the first few months of ownership. Then, of course, after a few years any car might need extensive repairs. Some large companies trade employee cars every three years or 36,000 miles, whichever comes first, because numerous repairs become necessary after this time.

About Cash Rebates, Now and Later

Federal law requires that car buyers who pay off loans early be given a refund on prepaid interest and insurance.

It works like this. Say you want to borrow $5,000 for your car and want to sign a note calling for payment in thirty-six months. Let's say that the interest and insurance over that period would amount to $1,250. Up front, the lender asks you to sign a note for $6,250, a combination of interest, insurance, and principal.

You find that you trade cars or can pay off the note in twenty-four months. Although you have signed up for thirty-six months of payments, you no longer owe the interest and insurance on those months. Just call your financial source and ask for the payoff figure on your loan, including interest and insurance rebates.

If in the past you have purchased credit life insurance, accident/ health insurance, collision insurance, or mechanical breakdown insurance, perhaps on your last car or the ones before that, and prepaid the loan, contact the insurance companies, banks, or dealerships to find out how much of a rebate is due you if you have not received one. This is all cash. It could amount to between a hundred and a thousand dollars. If you meet with resistance, it might indicate you ought to keep investigating.

And What about Manufacturers' or Factory Rebates?

Although these cash rebates are attractive to customers, especially when the auto-buying market is slow, they are not really healthy for the auto industry itself. The rebates, in effect, amount to borrowing from tomorrow's buyers. They steal from the future.

Of course you'll want to take advantage of rebate offers when they are available—who wouldn't?—but you should realize that the whole program of rebates and other "something for nothing" incentives will eventually cost us all.

Lowered interest rates and extended warranties provided by the manufacturers are actually forms of rebates. These and other rebate schemes are a gamble on the part of the manufacturer on the future reliability of their products. It is yet to be seen how much these will cost all of us in the long run.

The free extended warranties of the past, for instance, cost the manufacturers billions of dollars, and they have no way of retrieving that but passing the cost on to the customer. After Chrysler started these in order to survive, the other manufacturers followed suit as a competitive measure. All of them then had to raise prices to help cover the costs of their programs. The only glimmer of hope is that perhaps today's cars won't need as much service as the ones made in the '60s and '70s.

Deposits and Down Payments

Be willing—and able—to give a large deposit in order to show your good faith. A $100 to $1,000 deposit is not unreasonable. Your deposit might be your trade-in, even though a balance is owed on that trade-in to the finance company or bank. Don't ever be embarrassed that you finance your car! Remember that even Chrysler was financed—and by the United States government! In almost all cases you continue driving your trade-in until you pick up your new car.

Once you give a deposit and sign the purchase order, you have obligated yourself to buy the car at the terms specified. But what if you back out of the deal? Legally, in many states the dealer can keep your deposit or receive a percentage (such as 5 percent) of the full price of the car. So always write a "weasel clause" on the sales order if you have any doubts about your car purchase: "Subject to financing acceptable to buyer," or some other out.

Never let the salesman write "Cash" on the order unless you actually intend to pay cash, because you can be obligated to buy even if you cannot get the cash.

If a dealership cannot provide financing as agreed, they must give your deposit back—unless you have assented in writing to other conditions.

If you write a check for your deposit and then want a refund, a dealer will not give the deposit back until your check has cleared your bank.

A down payment is the total amount of value you put down when you actually purchase a car. It could be your old car or cash, or both, and will include your initial deposit. Dealers can even handle a vacant lot, a gold watch, or a cow—whatever has discernible value. Many financial institutions require a down payment of 25 to 30 percent of the purchase price. On the other hand, some dealerships may offer 100 percent financing (which might also be obtained from private individuals).

When you do make your down payment, be wary. The business manager or the finance and insurance manager might try to get additional money. Stick to the amount you have specified; it could be that the financial institution will only finance so much money on a particular car.

Some dealers might try to persuade you to sign a side note or give them a pickup payment (extra money, given later, to be applied to the down payment), if you can't get the deal otherwise. Actually, though, pickup payments, side notes, and postdated checks are not really legal, nor are dealer-arranged small loans. A customer should have *all* the down payment at the time of delivery, period. With 100 percent financing, they might ask you to pay sales tax, license and title fees, and/or your first and last car payments.

Since financing is occasionally arranged *before* a car is actually purchased, with money advanced to you, do keep the following situation in mind. Suppose you already borrowed some or all of the money for your car (which I don't recommend), but find that the model you want must be ordered, so that the delivery will take a while. Hang onto your money for the time being—don't turn it over to the dealer! The large sum you have borrowed should be left in your own account, to draw interest until your car arrives.

You can also consider "creative financing" and "creative banking" (see page 42). Sometimes that money can be put to use for other projects that you might have going for you. It's all in the way you approach banking and money.

Be cautious. In most cases you should not give anyone a deposit until your deal is acknowledged as acceptable to the seller and then signed as such by the dealer and his authorized agent or, in the case of a private party, by the car owner. However, many sales pros will tell you, "Money gets my manager excited . . . It gets his heart started."

Only you can decide when it's time to give a deposit.

Shopping Around for Interest Rates

When the cost of borrowing money is high, auto retail credit from some banks generally gets smothered. However, manufacturer finance sources (GMAC, Ford Credit, Chrysler Credit, World Omni, GE Credit, etc.) are in business for one purpose—to finance cars or trucks.

In 1981–1982, even with the prime rate at 20 percent, one company offered buyer financing on new cars at 13.8 percent. In many parts of the nation this offer met with great success. More recently, when two finance companies offered interest rates below 10 percent, auto sales boomed.

Be sure to shop for the best possible rate of interest. For instance, is there money to borrow from an old insurance policy— yours or a family member's—at 5, 6, or 7 percent? Or from a retirement trust . . . or a wealthy relative or benefactor? Options like these can save a lot of money.

And remember, if you're looking at used cars, the older a car is, the higher the rate of interest. So check how that affects long-term cost before you decide.

Whatever you arrange, make certain the interest rate is an *annual* percentage rate and not something else. People will often fall for a scam like "super-low" interest rates at 4.5 or 5.1 percent. This is always bait to get you inside the showroom. The only way to borrow money at 5 percent is from an old insurance policy or benevolent relatives who take you under their wing. The advertised low interest rates are cancelled out when the dealer adds the interest "savings" onto the price of the car.

Special Finance Plans for Special People

People working in certain professions get special breaks on financing, or at least special plans. Teachers and farmers are the main beneficiaries.

Teachers, who have no income during the summer vacation months, can get a financing plan that applies to the sale of new cars and models from the previous four years. Payments may be skipped for a maximum of four months in any year during the vacation period.

Regular new and used car finance charges are calculated as if consecutive monthly payments are being made, so the regular twelve-month equal payment finance charge would apply, with the amount of contract divided into eight or nine equal payments.

As for farmers, whose income is apt to be seasonal and erratic, installments may be scheduled in varying amounts to suit their convenience, provided their equity in the car (down payment plus installments paid) meets the necessary prearranged requirements.

Payment Schedules

Become familiar with payment schedules. Don't let an offer of "a car for only $9.17 a month extra" or some such attractive-sounding come-on get you to leap for a car deal before you evaluate total cost. That $9.17 a month could be at 18 percent interest and could last until Nellie has kittens—Nellie being your dog.

Don't sign any deal until you know the full story. For instance, if you *did* agree to the $9.17 a month payment, you must understand that this is really a figure per hundred dollars borrowed.

Time Periods and Interest Rates for Automobile Loans
(Figures are payments per $100 borrowed)

| % | Months | | | | |
	12	24	36	48	60
6	$8.61	$4.44	$3.05	$2.35	$1.94
7	8.66	4.48	3.09	2.40	1.99
8	8.70	4.53	3.14	2.45	2.03
9	8.75	4.57	3.18	2.49	2.08
10	8.80	4.62	3.23	2.54	2.13
11	8.84	4.67	3.28	2.59	2.18
12	8.89	4.71	3.33	2.64	2.23
13	8.94	4.76	3.37	2.69	2.28
14	8.98	4.81	3.42	2.74	2.33
15	9.03	4.85	3.47	2.79	2.38
16	9.08	4.90	3.52	2.84	2.44
17	9.13	4.95	3.57	2.89	2.49
18	9.17	5.00	3.62	2.94	2.54

Thus if you borrow $10,000 at $9.17 per hundred, your repayment would amount to $917 a month for twelve months (see table)—which you probably could not afford—or $254 per month for five years. The $254 figure certainly sounds better, but you should realize that by paying the higher amount over twelve months you would pay back $11,004 on the $10,000 for one year, whereas paying the lower amount over five years will mean that you will repay $15,240—or 50 percent more than the money you borrowed.

So you need to look at these money matters carefully. If anyone suggests what sounds like a fantastic deal to you, examine all aspects before you jump in. Always be sure to ask, "What is the *total* cost to me?"—and get the straight answer.

Payment schedules may vary according to the amount of interest you are paying and what down payment or trade-in you have, but a typical payment schedule appears on page 39. This shows the monthly payment you would make for each $100 lent to you.

For example, if you borrow $5,000 for four years at 15 percent interest, divide $5,000 by $100 to get 50 and then multiply by 2.79 (see table). Your monthly car payment would therefore be $139.50 plus any charges for insurance or warranty you may agree to include.

Period of Financing

You realize, of course, that the longer it takes you to pay off a conventional loan, the more cumulative interest you'll be paying. To conserve your hard-earned money, try to make the highest possible monthly payment within your means, in order to pay back the loan as swiftly as possible.

Some people, however, are less concerned about total cost than they are about the size of monthly installments, in which case they might well prefer a longer-term payment period.

When considering the duration of payments, keep in mind how many miles you drive each year. Assuming that you wait until your loan is fully paid off, you may find that your car has too many miles on it when you get ready to trade again.

Remember that the value of the average new car depreciates approximately 25 to 30 percent in the first year, 15 to 20 percent in the second year, and 10 to 15 percent in the third year. Exceptions to this are relatively few. However, some high-quality cars hold their initial price or actually increase in value because of inflation or demand. And though there is no sure way of predicting this, the body styles and mechanisms of some car models age so well through the years that eventually they will qualify as "antiques" or classics—for which collectors will pay large amounts of money, particularly if the car has been lovingly tended.

Ways to Buy the Car You Want

Suppose you have some cash on hand but cannot get financing for the car you really want because of a tight money market, lack of a good credit rating, or some other reason. Don't settle for a junker or any other car that does not meet your needs and with which you'll be unhappy before you even get it paid off. Innovative car-purchasing enterprise could well take you into the domain of creative financing, to be discussed shortly.

Obtaining Short-Term and Demand Notes

When purchasing a car, for the purpose of making a sizable down payment you could consider getting a short-term or demand note.

Short-term notes of sixty to ninety days can be arranged for minimal fees if you qualify. You will have to convince the lender that you have the ability to handle whatever you are borrowing in so short a time, and that you are not asking for a short-term note just to look more desirable as a borrower. If you qualify, your banker might even arrange for a ninety-day, six-month, or twelve-month signature or collateral short-term loan, so that you pay just the interest for the time being. Such a note can be renewed as many times as you and the bank agree to renew it. But these are generally demand notes, so you must have the means of coming up with the principal whenever or if ever it is demanded by the lender.

How's Your Credit Rating?

It's best, of course, to think about your credit needs well in advance of buying a car and then laying the groundwork for your future purchase.

Sooner or later, a good credit rating is important to attain. Strange as it may seem, you may have trouble getting car financing if you don't already have a record locally of repaying loans or regularly using charge accounts. This can even happen to thrifty people who have been long-time residents but prefer to pay cash.

Another kind of credit problem can surface from your deep dark past, when you were young and irresponsible or else ran into a period of tough financial times. Your adverse financial profile, which will be duly noted in various computer files to which potential creditors have immediate access, will now need to be revised. It will take effort, as many worthwhile things do, but in the end you will be able to not only buy a car but also establish your good name in the financial community where you live.

The following section shows how you can establish a good credit rating fairly quickly—and legitimately.

An Example of Creative Financing

Place a chunk of money in your savings account. For ease of computing, let's use $1,000 as the for-instance figure. You'll deposit it in an account that will pay you approximately 5.75 percent interest. And you'll make sure you can withdraw the money at any time.

In three or four days, go in and ask the loan officer of that same bank to lend you $1,000. Tell the officer you will put up your $1,000 savings passbook as collateral. Ask for six or twelve monthly payments to repay this loan.

Then deposit the second $1,000 (the one you got as a loan) in another bank. Wait three or four days and do the same thing all over again. Deposit the $1,000 from the second loan in a third bank. Wait three or four days and repeat the procedure, only this time use the proceeds from this third loan to pay off the loan at the first bank—not all at once but by making a payment weekly instead of every month. Being ahead of schedule in this way will impress the bank officers.

Plan to utilize your wages in paying off the other loans. If you can't pay them off comfortably on the terms the bank wants to arrange for you when you borrow, remember how much you can afford to pay and agree to payments only on that basis.

As you begin figuring how to accommodate future car payments, never lose sight that some additional expenses (insurance, fuel, maintenance) will accompany your car purchase.

When you have made monthly payments on a weekly basis for three to six months, make an appointment with the loan officer of the first bank. Ask if the bank can help you borrow $XXX—the total amount needed for your car. Show your payment record at that bank. If you can't get all you need from the first bank, your second and third banks should supply other avenues of credit.

Now, how much will the loan or loans actually cost you? Anywhere from 2 to 15 percent, depending on the number of loans and the interest rate over the rate of interest paid to you on your passbook savings. If you had one loan that cost you 3 percent, you would be out $30 interest, which is tax-deductible, and you have saved your $1,000. Whether you follow these precise directions or not, you should establish credit comfortably prior to buying a car by paying on something significant: a bank loan or a large appliance, perhaps. (A $50 stereo set won't get you very far!)

Everyone needs credit. You may find bankers amazingly receptive to your scheme, because deposits from other people's savings accounts loaned to you and deposited in your savings account allows the bank to borrow up to *five* times of that total amount. For instance, when one person approached a banker in the way suggested above, the banker said, "I won't lend you a thousand dollars. I'll lend you three thousand and you can add the extra two thousand to your thousand-dollar savings account, and we'll hold the passbook as collateral. You see, the three thousand dollars you deposit in a savings account with us gives our bank the borrowing power of fifteen thousand dollars."

That's how *both* borrower and lender can benefit in creative banking or financing.

How about a $1,000 Clunker?

What might happen if you purchased a $1,000 car instead of waiting to get the one you *really* wanted?

You would be out the $1,000, and you might have to spend $100 in repairs each month. Yet you would not have the car you really hoped to drive around—and could have afforded had you waited and gone about acquiring it in a creative way.

To continue with this sad tale: When you try to sell your $1,000 clunker, unless you're lucky or extremely talented at selling, you'll probably receive far less than what you paid for it. Perhaps—let's guess—only $200. And if you did spend $100 per month in repairs for six months, that's a total of $600. This adds up to a $1,400 loss.

On the other hand. . .had you saved $200 a month for six months, or $1,200, you would now have a total of $2,200 saved (that $1,200 plus the original $1,000). Add on to that the $600 you would have otherwise spent on repairs, and you'd have $2,800 instead of the mere $200 you received for your car—perhaps your only cash on hand now.

In addition, had you deposited your initial $1,000 in a savings account or money market certificate, you could have earned good interest to add to your fluid assets to make a healthy down payment on the car of your dreams.

So be wise. Plan your moves well ahead of buying!

What to Do if You Can't Make the Payments

If you don't make your payments, the financial institution (which could be the dealership) simply takes your car back by repossessing it. And you may be out whatever you have invested in it so far, plus being held responsible for any loss when your repossessed car is sold.

Consider too that you will lose your credit rating through nonpayment. That might hurt you more in the long run than losing your car.

You can best avoid repossession by carefully and realistically calculating the car payments you can afford to make based on your present income. Forget about rosy future prospects! Leave some room for unexpected expenses. And don't neglect to figure in any added insurance, fuel, and maintenance costs, particularly if you will have another car in the household to support.

The best-laid plans go awry at times. People lose their jobs, an emergency suddenly intrudes, or some other unforeseen circumstance depletes or deletes a steady income or available assets.

The best thing to do in the unhappy predicament of being unable to meet the next car payment is to alert the dealership or financial institution to your problem. If you are honest with them, they may find ways to help you avoid the embarrassment of repossession. For instance, they might arrange for you to pay only interest for a month or so.

But if you must give up your car, do so voluntarily and gracefully. Don't wait until a forced "repo" takes place.

Don't try to find something wrong with your car if you just can't afford to make the payments: That's bad faith on your part. Remember, anything you do that is even faintly unethical has a way of coming back to haunt you.

FOUR

Your Map for Car Shopping

Computer Carl took pride in his ability to remember things. He said he had a real photographic memory.

For his summer vacation he hightailed it up to Detroit to buy a new car. For years he had heard how much money people could save when they bought a car in a city that makes them.

"Hi. I drove up here to save some *real* money and to see the sights," was how he greeted the Motor City dealership. Carl's fast shuffle and glib tongue impressed the entire sales staff. They could spot a greenhorn right off.

Like a computer printout, Carl began rattling off a list of options. After he signed over the title to his car and took the wheel of the new one, he put on his Stetson and drove around to see the sights.

Back home a week later, having spent hundreds of dollars on motels, hotels, meals, and gasoline, Carl wheeled into Bull Motors. He bragged to old Bull, a billiards buddy, about all the money he had saved while having a vacation too.

Bull promptly showed Carl how the freight charge on car shipping nowadays was just the same wherever you were. . .that they could have sold him the same car for $500 less. . .and that the trade-in allowance for his old car was actually $1,500 less than they would have given him.

How so? Well, Bull explained it. Unified Freight now made the car price equal to Detroit's. Carl had somehow forgotten to get the custom interior and exterior that he thought he was getting—and so paid more than he should have. And furthermore, Hurricane Hetty, recently passing through that part of Texas, caused floods that damaged 2,800 cars and trucks, so that for a few weeks afterward, in replacing them, the used car inventories were wiped out, and the demand drove the price way up.

Computer Carl, in a state of shock, went out of the place with his tail between his legs.

If we all could go out and buy the cars that really delight us, regardless of cost, the automobile marketplace and industry would be very different indeed. But we live in a practical world where people generally must buy something they can afford as well as like. Obviously, then, cost is usually the major factor when deciding what kind of vehicle to acquire.

Having talked about money in the last chapter, let me now discuss exactly *what* you intend to buy. And how best to decide on its particulars.

Make a Shopping List

It's fairly obvious that shopping can be done far more efficiently with a well-prepared shopping list.

Your trip to the market will be easier, quicker, and less costly than if you go into a crowded store and then start to think about what you want. In making a car-shopping list, note first the features you *must* have, and *then* the ones that you might welcome if you could afford them.

What Sort of Vehicle for You?

Your biggest decisions, more than likely, have already been made: whether you are getting an ordinary car, a van, or a pickup truck. You'll also know whether you are going to be able to buy a luxury-class automobile or a high-priced performance car, instead of something more practical and economical.

But even if money is not a big problem to you, surely you'll still be looking for ways either to cut costs or get more features for your money.

The one on the left is the salesman, Tony the dealer is in the middle, but watch out for the salesman on the right!

Since performance cars (high-class sports cars), vans, and trucks are special categories unto themselves, I'll leave most recommendations in those classes up to specialists. Let's concentrate our attention on conventional cars and options.

You'll be deciding at first whether you want a sedan, station wagon, or hatchback; a large or small car; a two-door or a four-door; automatic transmission or stick shift.

You probably won't be able to make a final list in one sitting. You may wish to investigate issues like fuel economy and to ponder whether to buy an American- or foreign-made car. Before making a final decision, you could consult with a few authorities or respected publications for recommendations.

For your convenience, here's a checklist that you can duplicate and then mark up for your own purposes, perhaps adding features or options important to you.

Professional Checklist

I have decided to buy the following car, truck, or van. My shopping list is:

Car _____ Model number _____

2-door _____ 4-door _____ Station wagon _____

Exterior color _____ Color-coordinated interior _____

TRANSMISSION:

floor shift _____ 4-wheel drive _____

3-speed manual _____ 4-speed _____ 5-speed _____ Automatic _____

ENGINE:

2-cylinder _____ 4-cylinder _____ 6-cylinder _____ 8-cylinder _____

Diesel _____ Cubic inches _____ Liters _____

CARBURETOR:

1-barrel _____ 2-barrel _____ 4-barrel _____

OPTIONS:

Air conditioning _____ Radial tires _____ Tinted Glass _____

Tilt wheel _____ Custom wheels _____ Vinyl roof _____

Console _____ Custom trim package _____ Custom interior _____

50/50 seats _____ Vinyl/cloth/leather _____ Bucket seats _____

Power seats _____ Power steering _____ Power windows _____

Power brakes _____ Power door locks _____ Cruise control _____

Remote mirrors _____ Space-saver spare _____ Rustproofing _____

RADIO:

AM _____ AM/FM _____ AM/FM stereo _____ 8-track tape _____

Player _____ Cassette _____ CB _____ Special speakers _____

Rear speakers _____ Door speakers _____ Brand name _____

Dealer-installed _____ Later-installation _____

FINANCIAL:

Interest rate _____ Insurance _____ Bank _____

NOTES:

foreign or Domestic?

A major decision is whether to buy a domestic or an imported car.

When a car comes from abroad, you must be concerned about safety factors, about whether you can get the exact colors and options you want, and whether parts and service will be available in your locale.

You'll also have to live with an ethical decision. By purchasing a foreign make, you are—even if only in a very small way—helping to drain our economy of money that should be flowing into it. The automobile industry has been central to the American economy (and the Canadian as well). It has provided large-scale employment in many places, not just in Detroit. Diminished sales have serious repercussions.

fuel Economy

Oil shortages of the early 1970s ushered in a new era of automotive engineering and marketing. The years of the great gasoline glut—when an attendant would fill your tank with 25-cents-per-gallon gasoline, check your oil and water levels, clean your windshield unasked, and then thank you for your patronage—ended with a thud.

Americans, suddenly fearful about obtaining gasoline, began to realize what Europe and Asia had known for years: gasoline is actually a precious commodity.

Americans had to learn that there were more sensible ways of driving than traveling in a living room on wheels. Unless people could *afford* to pay astronomical prices for gasoline, they had to make fuel economy a main concern in choosing a car.

The situation has not changed much.

Nostalgia endures for those old days of gas-guzzling eight-cylinder superwonders. People still cling to the retirement dream of traveling the nation's highways in a two-bedroom motor home. Sales of recreational vehicles have picked up again and are anticipated to remain healthy for the next few years. But those times when millions of Americans took to the road in their R.V.s are probably gone forever.

Midget or Monster?

Your car will come in one of three main sizes, in good part depending on your commitment to fuel economy.

SMALL CARS

Compacts and subcompacts are not always the least expensive cars, in spite of their diminutive size.

Small cars have a length of about 148" to 175", a width of 62" to 68", a wheel base of 88" to 101", and a weight of 1,800 to 2,600 pounds. The rear seats rarely offer much leg room.

Small cars usually have four-cylinder engines that give the best fuel economy. They have been in great demand in the last dozen years because of the skyrocketing price of fuel. European and Japanese carmakers capitalized on their head start in designing and manufacturing these cars.

These cars perform best with manual transmissions. An automatic transmission is acceptable when the engine is large enough.

MEDIUM CARS

A medium-size automobile normally seats five or six people, though not with space to spare. The engine has either four or six cylinders, and has enough power for automatic transmission and air conditioning, yet still operates with fuel economy.

These cars customarily have a length of between 177" to 204". The width might be between 62" to 72", the wheel base between 105" to 114", and the weight between 2,500 to 3,800 pounds.

LARGE CARS

The usual overall dimensions of large cars are: length—212" to 221"; width—approximately 75"; wheel base—114" to 121". Their weight generally ranges between 3,600 to 4,000 pounds.

These cars carry five people in comfort. A number of the current models are now approaching the luxury class in price and features. The engines are six-cylinder or small V-8s.

A large car will travel farther on a tank of gasoline because of the larger capacity of the gas tank. It is more convenient for transporting families or a group. The ride is more comfortable because of the longer wheel base and weight distribution. Since it is heavier, it has greater stability and is safer in collisions. A large car usually has more storage space, leg room, head room, and shoulder room.

About Engine Size

The crucial matter in overall car size is clearly the engine size. A big engine, required in a large car, usually uses more fuel. In past decades, when unlimited power on the open highway was a paramount virtue in American cars and gasoline flowed like water, some luxurious car models had as many as twelve cylinders.

The dependably powerful V-8 engine eventually became standard equipment in many American cars. The international energy crisis changed that. Engineering advances have improved the fuel efficiency of larger engines while reducing the number of cylinders.

You should get an engine that will fit your everyday needs but that won't be overtaxed if you carry an occasional heavier load or travel in more difficult terrain. A standard four- or six-cylinder has plenty of power even when air conditioning is added. If, however, you want to pull a trailer, see what the car manual advises.

Fuel Economy for You

Considering how long you will end up keeping a new car, you should investigate thoroughly its fuel economy. Although most people *think* this is a good idea, not everybody approaches the matter sensibly or logically.

When you hear about a guy who gets fantastic mileage, you should ask, "To carry how many people?" For example, if a car that costs $9,000 gets 30 mpg with one person in it, keep in mind that this mileage could decrease appreciably in proportion to the number of passengers. If another car, priced at $7,500, delivers 20 mpg with six people in it, that's a total of 120 mpg (20 per person). Perhaps you should look at it that way if you really need a car that must regularly accommodate a large load of people or goods.

Since this car would cost less, you would also have lower car payments, with less interest due. So if you have co-workers or a family to transport, this obviously would be a far more efficient purchase than the car that has an impressive fuel economy for one person.

Also consider the type of driving you do. If it involves long trips, after which you must arrive fresh, unrumpled, and ready to do business, the lower mileage of a roomier, more substantial car should clearly be of less concern.

Remember also to compare the fuel consumption of a standard transmission (or "stick shift") larger car with a smaller car that has an automatic transmission. It's possible there'll be a trade-off in fuel economy, so if you're willing to forgo the convenience of an automatic transmission, you could take on a bigger size.

One thing is certain: The old idea that you had to buy an import in order to get fuel economy is no longer valid. Not so long ago, Chevrolet was advertising a model, the Malibu, that with a standard shift was supposed to get 20 mpg and sell for $5,000. Toyota Celica, at 19 mpg, sold for $6,389 at the same time, and Datsun, at 18.5 mpg, sold for $6,800. So look around before you assume that the imports have greater fuel economy.

Diesel engines, like many other things, were forced onto the market before they were ready. Unknown problems surfaced as people drove them, and now fewer diesel cars are purchased than in the past. The manufacturers are facing up to their obligation by extending warranties on almost all diesel engine components.

Although a diesel engine gives excellent fuel mileage, service stations with diesel pumps may be hard to find. These engines also need routine servicing more often than gasoline engines. Other drawbacks: They are harder to start in cold weather, have less power, and are notoriously noisy.

For years, inventors of all kinds have fiddled around with devising new and better ways to power vehicles, and the compulsion to achieve something better than the internal combustion engine has been much accelerated. Now research and development staffs in large corporations, as well as garage tinkerers eager to make a fortune, are in on the search.

Be leery of investing in anything other than the conventional gasoline-using vehicle—no matter how exciting or promising its innovative engine seems. Wait until the noble experiment of running a car on sunlight or soybean oil or fermented cornhusks has been well proven!

I should have bought an in-line fuel heater.

Body Styles

Most cars are available in both two-door and four-door models. The four-door cars offer more leg room and are obviously easier to get in and out of. Generally they cost on the order of $50 more than the two-door version. Since they are a bit heavier, their fuel consumption can be expected to be somewhat higher too.

Station wagons are available in many models. Compared with sedans of a comparable overall body size, they have a larger carrying ability. They are good choices for those who regularly transport five or more passengers or often carry baggage.

A popular and sensible alternative to the station wagon is the hatchback, which sacrifices the conventional trunk to provide extra space for cargo. The rear seat of a hatchback can be folded down to provide a longer cargo floor.

What Are Your Options?

These are the main categories of choice when selecting features on a car:

TRANSMISSION

A manual transmission usually achieves better mileage than an automatic. In some cases it makes a dramatic difference indeed. Automatic transmission design has been changed on many new medium-size and large domestic cars so as to improve fuel economy. The difference, however, is minimal when compared with that of the stick shift's gas conservation. Read the manufacturers' claims, but always check the latest impartial test results.

Undeniably, it is easier for most people in ordinary street and road conditions to drive cars with automatic transmissions. This is particularly true when the driver has numerous distractions, or if much of the driving takes place on city streets under constant start-and-stop conditions. Furthermore, someone who has been driving with an automatic transmission for many years may find it extremely trying (and dangerous) to learn the other method and change driving styles.

As an additional option in many transmission systems, there is what is called cruise control or automatic speed control. It helps you to maintain a steady speed and hence improves your gas mileage. It disengages when you touch the brake or clutch pedal. WARNING: Cruise control may cause you to become so lulled by the effortless driving that you become inattentive to the road, especially when you are tired.

POWER BRAKES AND POWER STEERING

Power brakes are becoming standard on most cars. The brake pedal is lower and more convenient to use. In addition, disc brakes have become a popular feature because they allow easier servicing, quick stopping, and other safety benefits.

Power steering is also standard equipment on large and many medium-size cars. It is generally unnecessary on most small cars. Its effect on gas mileage is minimal.

AIR CONDITIONING AND HEATING

Air conditioning will increase the cost of repairs and will also cut gas mileage. But it may more than make up for these drawbacks by appreciably delaying or diminishing your fatigue. For people who must arrive at appointments in fresh condition and good spirits, an air conditioner should rightfully be considered a wise business investment. In many sections of the United States, it is a must nowadays. An integrated (factory-installed) air conditioner helps window defogging and fresh air circulation. This option will add to the resale value of a car.

Heaters are standard, built-in equipment in cars. In long vehicles such as station wagons and vans, a rear heater can be an option.

TIRES

Radial tires are standard on most new cars. The previous bias or belted tires (in which the cord runs the width of the tires instead of the length) had an average life of 25,000 miles. Radial tires (in which the cord runs crisscross) have a life expectancy of 50,000 miles.

Radial tires can stop quickly and handle wet surfaces with almost no loss of gripping power. The prime safety defect of most older tires was weakness in the sidewalls. A radial tire's sidewalls are much stronger.

Steel-belted radial tires give added strength and safety over plain radial tires because of the stronger steel cord.

WARNING: Never mix steel-belted radial tires with bias tires because of the danger when you brake.

Tires are generally plain black, but white walls add some cosmetic value, while white lettered tires make for a sportier appearance.

The compact or space-saver spare tire is an emergency tire that will get you to the nearest service station. Two popular designs are the solid rubber or the inflatable space-savers. WARNING: Read the instructions carefully if you use the inflatable space-saver. A conventional spare tire is still the best.

You can choose from a wide variety of hubcaps, wheels, and wheel covers—just fit the wheels to your particular budget and taste.

WINDOWS AND WINDOWGLASS

Tinted glass windshields have become standard on many cars. They function as an extra pair of sunglasses for the driver—and passengers too. These windows are mandatory for cars equipped with air conditioning because they help reduce the amount of work that the air conditioner must do on a sunny day. If you choose, dealerships will have outside companies shade your windows similar to those in many limousines.

Rear window wipers are standard on some imports and domestic compacts and subcompacts. They are available on some station wagons and hatchbacks, where they are particularly useful in improving visibility.

Defrosters and defoggers are both effective safety features in a car. Defrosters prevent the buildup of vision-impairing moisture on the inside of the windows; defoggers remove ice crystals that have formed on the windshield and rear window. Electronically heated rear window defoggers are best, but an electrically operated blower will do. Defoggers can also cause a drain on the battery.

POWER WINDOWS AND POWER DOOR LOCKS

Power windows offer convenience and add to the resale value of a car. But you must learn how to operate them properly. Also—something that people tend to forget about—it's awkward and even unpleasant, when the car's engine is turned off and the driver is away, if waiting passengers cannot regulate the air supply themselves by manually lowering or raising the windows.

If you have small children, you should first find out whether the car you plan to buy with power windows can be equipped with rear window safety locks. Young children if not closely tended will often play with the windows, and sometimes get their heads or hands caught in them.

Power door locks provide a central locking system in a car. With the touch of one button, you can lock or unlock all doors.

CAR LIGHTS

Manufacturers offer various headlight designs, depending on the model car, such as single headlights and dual headlights, which can be horizontal or stacked (one on top of the other). Headlights that are round in design have been the standard of the industry. And now there are rectangular headlights that are sometimes halogen (gas-filled, high candlelight-rated). They are all electric—they just take different approaches.

Emergency lights are standard on cars nowadays. They are controlled manually by a hazard switch that is usually located on the side of the steering column. They flash off and on to let others know you have problems.

Taillights and backup lights are standard. Taillights allow drivers behind you to see your car in the dark. When you step on the brake pedal, they glow brighter. The white backup lights warn drivers that you are backing up; they also light the area you are backing into.

Fog lights can be installed if heavy fog is a frequent condition in your area. Check with the local police to find out whether they are legal.

Parking lights with an automatic shutoff timer are available on some cars. The headlights and/or interior lights stay on for a while to give you time to get into your home. (But to make sure they go off, you might find yourself standing in the door for what seems like an hour.)

Courtesy lights are also useful. These lights automatically flash on when you open a door, glove compartment, hood, or trunk.

SEATS

A one-piece front (bench) seat, standard in many models, is comfortable when three people are sitting on it—unless there is a transmission hump. The so-called 50/50 seats, sometimes also known as 40/60 seats or bucket seats, are very good for couples who combine a short-legged driver with a long-legged front-seat passenger, or vice versa. They provide better support for two people, but become difficult if not impossible for three if there is a gear-shift box between the seats.

Power seats can be very helpful to short people who alternate with taller people in driving a car. They can also reduce driver fatigue, particularly on long trips, since periodic seat readjustment can change the pressure on your back and legs.

If you take many long trips, you might want to purchase reclining seats. These can be adjusted manually for comfort and relaxation, not to mention savings on motel bills if you can pull off the road and sleep a few hours to break up a lengthy, tiring drive. They also allow your companion in the front seat to nap, so that taking turns driving on a long trip goes easier.

Both power seats and bucket seats add to the resale value of a car.

UPHOLSTERY

Many people approach car upholstery looking for durability and resistance to soiling. Cloth upholstery is more likely to stain and harder to clean than the tougher materials, leather and vinyl. But with cloth you won't feel clammy in the summertime or cold in the winter—common complaints with the other two choices.

The plusher the cloth interior, the more susceptible it will be to staining, burns, and scratches. Overall, however, cloth, vinyl, and leather are equally durable. Vinyl seats are standard on most cars. Ordinary cloth interiors cost approximately $50 more, while luxury cloth interiors may cost hundreds of dollars more. Leather seats can cost approximately $500 more.

Regardless of material, when selecting upholstery keep in mind the heat-absorbing and heat-reflecting properties of dark and light colors. If you live in an area with strong sunlight through much of the year, a dark color is probably not advisable, since it absorbs and retains the sun's heat. You can reduce this hot-seat problem, however, by covering the upholstery whenever you park for any length of time outdoors during the day.

Floor mats are available from the manufacturer, dealer, or any "after-market" source.

Interior trim packages or deluxe interiors are available as factory options on many models. They might include plush carpeting, fancier side door panels and instrument panel, and seat upholstery like deep crushed velour.

BODY TRIM

Moldings on the body of your new car may not be standard, but you should consider buying them as a protection from banging or scraping—which is the real reason for these decorative features. (For decoration alone, you can purchase kits and glue on plastic that looks like metal.)

BUMPERS, SUNROOFS, AND LUGGAGE RACKS

All manufactured cars have bumpers, though many of the sporty models have one-piece bumpers made of plastic, endura, or rubber. Bumpers are placed so that they can meet another car's bumpers, front or back, on impact.

If you live, work, or drive (and park) in a large city or congested area, full-width bumper strips or facings and bumper guards are very helpful. They are optional in some areas but required by law in California and other states and cities.

A vinyl roof is a frill, but a *nice* frill. Remember, though, that vinyl, if not properly cared for, may deteriorate faster than a metal roof.

A sunroof lets in extra light and, when opened, increases air circulation—an important consideration, especially if you have no air conditioning. Bear in mind that a sunroof may reduce head room, a problem for tall people.

Both vinyl roofs and sunroofs add to the resale value of a car.

You'll find racks installed on many station wagon roofs and small-car trunk lids. Racks help carry excess luggage or long, oddly shaped items such as skis that cannot be accommodated in the trunk. If you fill the rack and drive at freeway speed, fuel economy will drop and handling will be a little more difficult.

Remember, however, that a variety of strap-on racks and luggage holders can be purchased later in auto supply stores and department stores, probably at considerably less cost than what you would pay the dealer. They are also available at equipment rental places, for use as needed.

AUDIO EQUIPMENT

Here you have to make a complicated choice: Do you want plain old AM, or AM/FM? An AM/FM stereo, or AM/FM/stereo/tape deck (cassette) player. . .or even a CB transceiver?

It isn't always possible to have a radio combo installed by the manufacturer. Dealers often order their stock cars or special cars without radios or with simple AM radios only. This should not be a major problem to you, however, even though it might have been convenient to get a package audio deal with the car.

Although a better radio doesn't add much to the trade-in value, it will provide you with undeniably improved listening pleasure. Special additional audio features, however, do increase the resale value, since many car buyers these days are also audio buffs.

Actually, you can invest in a minimal sound system and then add to it as your tastes and knowledge develop. A number of audio equipment and auto supply stores carry do-it-yourself audio systems for cars, often at discount prices that may be considerably lower than a "deal" given to you by a dealer. Be aware of this possibility, anyway, during a bargaining session, and perhaps go beforehand on your own to price independently installed systems.

An outside antenna, instead of one molded onto the window, will improve your reception. (And people who regularly park in huge lots often use them, of course, as handy flagpoles to carry prominent identifying markers.) A power antenna, which costs about $100 more, is a convenience and ensures against vandalism, for it rises only when the radio is on. If you buy a power antenna, be sure to turn off the radio when you go through a car wash.

TRAILER-TOWING PACKAGE

This is a must for anyone who regularly tows a trailer. It has an upgraded electrical system and the wiring necessary for providing the lighting on a trailer.

Keep in mind that many of today's cars are not powerful enough to pull heavy loads. Someday, because of the decreasing horsepower available in engines built to save fuel, the only vehicles capable of towing such loads safely may be trucks or recreational vehicles.

Now let's move on and talk about how much your new vehicle should realistically *cost* you.

Sticker shock is stabilizing.

FIVE

Figuring on the Price

Daring David asked his Indiana banker, Tight Fist, for the dealer cost of the new midsize car, Fishtail, that he wanted to buy. Then he headed for his choice of dealerships.

He knew that he would not impress a salesman by trying to act sharp and telling him, "I know your ten-thousand-dollar car only costs you eighty-five hundred." David realized this would create an invisible barrier between them, and perhaps even send the salesman to the manager to say, "I've got a smart———out here. Can you have someone else help him?"

Glad Hand, the salesman, greeted Daring David by opening the door to the showroom and saying, "Welcome to Rose Garden Motors." Glad Hand's charisma guided David through the sales presentation. Then the pricing duel began.

"How much?" David asked. Glad Hand, smiling, told him, "Ten thousand dollars." David said softly, "I told you I want to buy a car today. . . . Look, I don't want you to lose money. . . . How much?"

After further negotiations and a lot of "Aw, come ons" and long silences from David, Glad Hand came down to $9,000.

David then said, "I want your best deal right now." But Glad Hand would not go below that $9,000. Daring David, though, had been told by Tight Fist that salesmen stop at what they consider a minimum deal and then really start selling hard. "They will try everything they know on you at this point," he had said.

Remembering this, David said firmly, "Glad Hand, I want to buy a car today. . . . I'll give you eighty-five fifty." He knew he was wearing Glad Hand down.

They finally agreed on $8,625.

This was the beginning of a relationship that lasted for many years. Daring David bought eight more cars, and he also referred many people to Glad Hand.

Glad Hand tells other salesmen, "Daring David is always hard to sell. But sooner or later, I get him. And he's my best bird dog, too."

Most people conclude that the best deal is not necessarily the lowest price, because convenience, terms, trade-in value, and a good service department are all important variables when making a decision. Some buyers are willing to pay a hundred dollars or more just to be assured of good service.

Only by shrewd negotiating can you determine your best deal. Read on. . .and discover how to buy at the lowest possible price.

What's a Sticker Price?

The sticker price is merely a manufacturer's *suggested* list price. A dealer can discount the price or add $1,500, $4,000, or any other amount he decides on.

In the case of a hot seller, as was a low-volume production like the Corvette Indianapolis pace car, some dealers added as much as $12,000 to the $18,000 sticker price. And some people actually *paid* $30,000. Just as beauty is in the eye of the beholder, so is value. Some clients who had read about the Special Limited Production Corvette in auto magazines were offering dealers $12,000 to $25,000 before the car was introduced.

Dealerships or salesmen will sometimes also add their *own* sticker price to the preexisting one, an extremely irritating practice. When the customer is looking at a very popular, hot-selling model and trying to bargain, a salesman may say, "If you don't pay our price, someone else will." The best way to change his tune is to say, "Fine, sell it to someone else then." After that, just walk out. Period.

Prices for Used Cars

Many dealers mark up their used cars with a $1,500 to $5,000 profit margin, or even more. This all depends on the type of car. High-line specialty cars have the higher margin. However, some dealers would be willing to sell you a particular used car at their actual cost or even less. It could be a "don't-wanter"—one in stock too long—or the value could have dropped quickly. Or the appraiser could have misappraised the car, giving it too high a value.

Financial institutions, newspaper ads, and wholesale used car price publications can give you an approximate *current market value,* in both wholesale and retail figures. But please remember: No two used cars are identical, whether you are buying or selling.

Getting Professional Price Assessments

One way of getting a reasonable price assessment—maybe the lowest—is to write a letter on good stationery and send it to five different dealerships handling the same brand of car. Address it to the Fleet Department or the Fleet Manager and say you are interested in a specific car with specifically named equipment. Give your name, address, and phone number, and ask for a fleet bid. They won't know if you're a doctor or attorney, but the good stationery will suggest that you might be. All you need is one very low offer. Of course, you can't do this more than once, and the bid may not be the lowest available price.

Your friendly local banker or credit union representative knows the dealer's cost for a new car. People in positions to arrange for car financing are able to determine whether a buyer is paying a fair price. Maybe you're already acquainted with someone who has ready access to such information. If not, get close to a financial consultant by dropping in for a visit and perhaps offering to share some refreshment with him or her.

At an opportune time, ask what the particular new model you're already interested in costs a dealer and what the list price is. And as long as you're there, you could also ask what this financial adviser thinks of the retail and wholesale value of your present car, including extras and mileage allowances, if you're going to be using it as a trade-in. Unless you are buying a used car, you won't be interested in loan value—the index banks use to decide how much money to loan you on a particular used car. But realize that listed used car prices are only ballpark guidelines. The real prices are decided at the auto auctions.

Remember that there are other ways to discover the dealer's costs for your prospective car and the trade-in value of your old car. Use the figures and the procedures outlined in *Consumer Reports* or the price books on new and used cars that are available at bookstores, newsstands, and libraries.

For a small fee you can also find out dealer costs from national computer printouts. Two sources are:

Nationwide Auto Brokers   Toll-free number 1-800-521-7257
17517 W. Ten Mile Road   Michigan residents
Southfield, MI 48075   1-313-559-6661

Car-puter   Toll-free number 1-800-221-4001
1603 Bushwick Ave.   New York metro area 1-718-455-2500
Brooklyn, NY 11207

Calculating the Dealer Markup

Many years ago, dealers had uniform 25 percent discount structures from their auto manufacturers. But automakers gradually lowered the profit margin between dealer cost prices and manufacturers' suggested list prices.

Today, small cars, compacts, and subcompacts have approximately a 10 percent range plus destination charges and an advertising co-op charge of about $20 to $70. (Advertising co-op charges derive from deals automakers have struck with their dealers, who agree to advertise as a group, with each dealer paying $20 to $70 for each car sold toward the ads: the manufacturer adds this fee to the dealer's invoice and so passes the cost to the consumer.) Markups may vary depending on the make, model, and area in which a dealer is located. Intermediate-size models have about a 14 percent markup while 15 percent is the norm on luxury models. Some special low-volume luxury cars have a 25 percent markup. Factory-installed options have a margin of approximately 15 percent.

Keep in mind, though, that the customary percentage of markup between list and cost can change the day after this book is published!

Let's make some sample calculations in figuring out a particular dealer markup. Say the manufacturer's *suggested* list price of a subcompact is $8,410—including $600 in options and $310 for freight charges. However, as you can find out at the bank or credit union, or from a current sourcebook, the total dealer or base cost is:

factory-suggested retail price	$7,500
less 10% dealer discount	− 750
dealer cost	$6,750
factory options	$600
less 15% dealer discount	− 90
cost of options	$510
dealer (base) cost	$6,750
plus options	510
plus freight	310
plus advertising	30
COST TO DEALER	$7,600

In this case, you can see that the dealer has more than $800 worth of gross profit built into this suggested list price, instead of the presumed 10 percent.

The average gross profit to a dealer on a car sale is about $700, including the dealer's holdback and after-market sales (as explained later) plus finance and insurance income. However, high floor plan costs because of high interest rates can eliminate the income from the finance and insurance areas.

And who knows? Maybe the manufacturers will continue to narrow the gap between list price and the initial cost—to make the list price increasingly a fair trade price. Such a situation would make considerable changes, of course, in dealership profit-making tactics and in buyer/seller negotiations.

For Those Who Buy Expensive Cars

For years American cars followed the same basic evolving design. Price was the essential distinction. The original luxury car buyer was fulfilling a desire to drive a status symbol, a car that few others could afford. High demand for low volume meant high price.

When the American automakers produced the Cadillac, Lincoln, and Chrysler, they intended to satisfy luxury-class needs. Then they fashioned their volume lines—Chevrolet, Ford, and Plymouth—to resemble their more luxurious cousins. Thus they catered quite democratically to the dreams and desires of all car buffs.

After a while, even many Charlie and Mary Lunchbuckets, the foundations of our economy, began purchasing somewhat more luxurious cars when their incomes permitted it. They reasoned that it made little sense to buy car "G" when they could get car "L" for the same monthly payment. They just financed the balance over a longer period of time. This extension of payment time also helped used car buyers become new car owners.

When the "common people" began to invade the once-exclusive domain of higher-priced American-made automobiles, many wealthy people or "high rollers" searched for new status symbols. For many, the desirable new cars were foreign, with names like Rolls-Royce, Jaguar, Mercedes-Benz, Porsche, and BMW. Their production and exportation limited, these cars were not readily available, and often cost much more than their American equivalents in size and appearance.

Then it happened again: More and more Americans somehow managed to purchase the latest in highly visible status symbols. Now many wealthy people are seeking to buy even more elite and expensive cars, which they trust will display their uniqueness for a while at least. Today's sophisticated wealthy buyers, however, look at *both* price and perceived value. They go after a car that is as close to perfection as possible.

The Rolls-Royce and Mercedes-Benz automobiles, by reputation, are superb, high-quality cars. The United States has been Rolls-Royce's most important export market. In 1981 Rolls-Royce was looking at record sales of 1,300 Rolls and Bentley cars in the United States. In 1983 the stripped-down Silver Spirit sold for $99,695 and the Silver Spur for $110,295. The less expensive but nonetheless elitist Mercedes-Benz exported 63,059 vehicles to the United States in 1981, followed by 65,963 in 1982.

The elite car market, with its low sales volume and high prices, was traditionally a small segment of a very large international marketplace. Domestic manufacturers simply had not been concerned with it. They focused instead on producing luxurious-*looking* automobiles in higher volume, priced so more people could afford them.

However, 66,000 cars sold in the United States by just one foreign manufacturer is a substantial amount. And $117,000 for a single car is not to be sniffed at either. In hindsight it was foolish that Cadillac, Lincoln, and Chrysler did not also design and produce more exclusive models.

Gray Market Cars

Many lawsuits have developed in some areas of the country over "gray market" cars. This slightly tainted business expanded tremendously in the early and mid '80s, with the ravenous demand for hot-selling European imports, such as BMW, Mercedes and Porsche.

People buy gray market cars to get immediate delivery, thinking their car will be identical to a fully inspected new car import. They're wrong. Gray market cars are not built to American standards: the tires are not the same tires, frame is not the same frame, etc. Glass, tires, body, frame, bumpers, and pollution controls usually don't conform with U.S. safety standards and regulations.

How do gray market cars reach our country? Some are factory-official used cars, while others are indeed new, purchased direct from a European dealer and "laundered" through independent used car dealers who have pollution controls and bumpers changed, but leave other parts alone. Many are stolen or used cars.

New York State is combating the gray market car by refusing to issue a New York car title if a new car does not have a certificate of origin.

What Price Prestige and Perfection?

The Rolls-Royce is supposedly the standard of excellence. But they still give you a guarantee and a warranty when you buy one— which means that there may be flaws in the manufacturing.

So what is perfection? Can you and I really afford to buy a "perfect" car? (I'll admit *I* can't!)

Remember that any repairs or parts replacements on elite-class cars from abroad will cost you more than the same labor or part on a domestic car. Not only do you pay more for the imported parts themselves, but you often have to wait while they are obtained from a distant distributor. Furthermore, labor generally is more expensive.

But it is often hard to persuade people to be more sensible when it comes to status-seeking.

Take my old friend Dapper Dan. A few years ago, Dan told me that he had been trying to buy a new Mercedes and was going to sell his '78 model. Several months earlier, while in Germany on business, he had tried to buy one but was told that individuals wanting American specifications would have to wait eighteen to twenty-four months for delivery. And when he tried to buy one through a business associate in Italy, he was given the same answer. The Mercedes dealers in the United States obviously had the export situation tied up.

At the time Dan and I talked, the Mercedes would have cost him $33,000 if purchased in Germany. But it would have cost him $25,000 earlier, when he initially tried to get it, because of the higher value of the American dollar versus the deutsche mark at that time. (Overnight shipping by air freight would have cost him an additional $900.)

This same car would cost Dan $48,000 in the United States. But it turned out that neither of the two local Mercedes dealers had one in stock. A dismayed Dan was told he would be put on a waiting list to buy a car that someone else had ordered but didn't take after all.

Now, Dan, like most other people, was an impulse buyer. He had to have a car *right now,* with the equipment he wanted and in his favorite color. Frustrated, he even looked at a new Rolls-Royce for $110,000. And a '79 with 16,000 miles for "only" $60,000—but it was yellow and green, not his favorite colors. Also, he felt he didn't fit with this type of car, in which he should really be chauffeured around. Dan, who usually just pulled out his checkbook and drove a car home, didn't . . . this time.

As we talked, Dan mentioned that Mercedes dealers probably average a $5,000 profit per car—which seemed rather excessive to both of us (though I reminded Dan that making a profit is not a sin). He admitted that his main reason for owning a Mercedes was to experience the prestige of driving an automobile that few people around him could afford to own. He also knew that Mercedes owners become hooked on that car, even though it has fewer luxurious features than the high-line domestic cars. And despite his wife's dislike for driving the older Mercedes they owned (she preferred their Eldorado), Dan intended to buy a brand-new sedan anyway.

I then showed Dan how much money he could save by buying a $20,000 domestic luxury car instead of the $48,000 elite-class import. First, the higher-priced import car dealers—Mercedes, Porsche, and the like—haven't discounted cars to the consumer to the extent domestic dealers have—Cadillac, Lincoln, Chrysler, Oldsmobile—who are willing to negotiate with informed buyers to as low as $100 to $1,000 over cost. (However, 1985 did find some import dealers willing to negotiate for the first time in several years, though each sale still averaged $4,000 profit over cost.)

Dan also knew the tax deduction laws of 1984 militated against buying an expensive import. The new tax law allows for normal income tax deduction on cars used for business purposes—a maximum depreciation of $4,000 per year—*if* that car cost approximately $16,000 or *less*. Cars priced over that range would be depreciated over a longer period of time.

I also pointed out to Dan that he could invest his savings into a profit-making venture and that a domestic luxury car would cost him less for service and parts. Dan knew, of course, that the cost of interest on a loan for a $48,000 car will be much higher than that for a $20,000 car.

In effect, Dan could drive the lower-priced but nonetheless prestigious car at no cost (other than gas, insurance, and maintenance), plus have the advantage of depreciation and tax shelters if he chose to.

But past a certain point you can't do much to shake a determined car buyer. Soon after I talked with him, Dan went out and bought a $48,000 Mercedes sedan.

You might ask, though, why the dealer with a $48,000 car proved unwilling to give my car-buying friend Dan a discount, whereas the dealer with the $20,000 car would have given him a healthy one. The answer once again: the old law of supply and demand.

Times Are Changing

For years, American cars were built to go out of style. The American emphasis on constant consumerism was as prevalent in the automobile marketplace as it was in the fashion industry. With intentionally redesigned, radically new car models introduced every two or three years, the old-style car was not the "in" thing.

The rapid styling changes quickly made current models outmoded. The manufacturers created their own fashions, but they also borrowed what had proved popular with their competitors.

Unfortunately for all of us, domestic automakers were not interested in developing the small car market because profit margins were too low. In the '50s and '60s they let Volkswagen supply small cars to the comparatively few buyers who wanted them.

As late as 1982, the Japanese were able to capture 22.5 percent of sales because domestic carmakers could not produce acceptable small cars in large volume. And the desire for small cars will not disappear. Conspicuous consumption is on the wane. In an ecologically minded and increasingly cost-conscious society, more and more consumers insist upon durability, safety, longevity, space saving, quality performance in products—particularly in high-cost products like cars!

SIX

Learning about Dealers

Missouri's Go-Getting Charlie, in his first three months as a car dealer, won a trip to the Orient for selling his dealership's factory quota. Still excited after the vacation, he went directly to the agency as soon as he got off the plane.

This unexpected morning entrance found two salespeople and a mechanic leaning on the parts counter discussing the World Series with three parts employees—while two customers screamed at the service manager. What a welcome home! But that was just the start.

Upon entering the showroom, Charlie saw a group of salesmen eyeing and discussing the women waiting at the bus stop outside. Two others were reading the newspaper, while one man leaned back in his chair, face toward the ceiling, snoring up a storm. Still another group sat around complaining about the local economy.

But if business wasn't coming in the door, Charlie asked, why weren't they out *looking* for some?

Approaching the sales office now, Charlie with some relief saw his sales manager in serious conversation with two other managers and several salespeople. He came in unnoticed—and learned that their healthy business conversation was about organizing a weekly football pool.

Now that he was back, Charlie realized he must get all his employees quickly into shape again if he was going to have any more free and fancy trips. He called for a meeting of the entire staff, to discuss telephone prospecting. He selected Red Turkey, the most talkative and gregarious salesperson, to be the first to make a "cold" call. Amplifying the two-way conversation would demonstrate to the others how it should be done.

Unaccountably nervous, Red Turkey dialed the number selected at random from the phone book, and when a lady answered he suddenly choked up and was speechless. He had to hang up. Go-Getting Charlie was horrified and told him so. Red admitted now that all ten of his required daily phone-prospecting calls were to the weather and time reports or to his home. Somehow, he just couldn't talk on the phone!

Charlie instructed Red to do his cold prospecting from now on in person, at places of business. All he had to do was get them to sign a note acknowledging that he had come in to sell cars. His sales tripled in a month.

By keeping his eye on improving employee motivation and encouraging techniques styled for individual sales talents, Charlie saw to it that his salespeople soon began taking incentive trips themselves. And in a half year he flew off on another all-expenses-paid, factory-sponsored vacation—this time to Europe.

Anyone who wants to buy a new car should deal with a franchised dealership.

By now you have figured out how much money you can spend on a car and how you'll obtain it, what features are important to you, and the kinds of cars you are most interested in. You have pretty much filled in your car-shopping list. But you may not have determined exactly where you're going to look for your car-to-be. And you are not sure yet how to do it, especially when it comes to talking with salesmen and dealers.

Those are the two big issues we'll consider in the next three chapters: choosing the right dealership for you and handling the sales situation advantageously.

Auto Dealers come in all shapes and sizes. They have a common interest in cars, satisfied customers, people, and making money. Many are involved in other businesses. They are human beings. They breathe, bleed, and actually die.

Finding a Good Deal at a Good Dealership

You might save up to $5,000 by choosing the right dealer. Postpurchase service is another major factor in dealer choice. So obviously you'll want to put some time and effort into the selection process.

Knowing which dealership to do business with is a problem for most car buyers.

You may want to stick with the dealer from whom you bought your last car, perhaps because he has been servicing it ever since. But ponder the situation carefully. Are you really so happy with the relationship that you want to continue it? Do you feel that you may be taken for granted there—and that they might not put much effort into making a car deal sweet for you? Maybe another dealer would appreciate your business more and therefore would offer you a more attractive package. After all, it's your money and you should not feel that you owe a past dealer any strong loyalty.

In any event, investigate all the dealerships in your area that handle the cars that interest you.

Talk to your friends and neighbors about their experiences with the kinds of cars you're considering and also about their local dealers' reputations. Also try to talk with anyone who drives a car of interest to you that shows a local dealership's license holder.

Call your local consumer agency or Better Business Bureau to get recommendations—and warnings. Find out any complaints that are registered against a dealer. But also ask how old these complaints are, for a dealer may have overcome an undeserved reputation that perhaps was caused by an inept or unethical employee.

If and when you do find a dealership that treats you fairly and courteously and gives you good service, tell all your friends and acquaintances about it. Virtues like these need all the reinforcements and rewards they can get.

Friend or Foe?

You can often learn from your own personal experience or by hearing about someone else's. For instance, I recently purchased a car, and the lowest interest rate available—from the nation's largest automobile finance company—was 13.75 percent APR (that's the annual percentage rate, or "real interest"). But I looked around and found a local bank that would lend the same money at 11.75 percent. This saving of 2 percent interest per year on a three-year loan saved me approximately $700. Moreover, my insurance agent, using a different insurance company, combined my homeowner's and automobile insurance policies and thereby reduced my insurance premiums from $1,600 to $975—a savings of over $600. So always be on the lookout for cheap money.

Still, shopping for the best price on a car can be tricky, even for an old hand like me. Intending to buy a new car, I decided to purchase one from a dealer friend I've long known and trusted. He had an outstanding personal reputation, as did his business. Relying on the virtue of this connection, I didn't even go to any other dealerships to look around. And he, of course, had assured me that I would get the best possible deal. So I came in on a Friday, looked at his cars, told him which one I wanted, and said I'd be back in a couple of days to pick it up. When I came in—all the financing arranged, ready to drive it away—I saw it was not the car I had picked out, though it was the same color. This one had 2,000 miles on it, vinyl roof, and less equipment. I knew the other car had been brand-new. I had also written down its serial number, so now I checked it to make sure. The number on this car was different.

Stunned, I thought quickly about why they were trying to foist this car on me. Perhaps when choosing I had seemed to be in such a hurry that it was assumed that I had not looked closely at the car I had selected, which was one of their hot-selling items. I began to piece together what might have transpired after I left. Hearing that the dealer would be selling me the car at his cost, the manager could have said, "My gosh, we can't get enough of these cars. How come you're selling it at this price? Can't you sell him something else?" Or maybe someone else came in and wanted to buy that particular car right away, at their asking price, without any haggling. Or else one of the managers was given that same car to drive as a demonstrator, while the car he had been driving was simply presented to me, in the certainty that I wouldn't notice. They could justify this substitution by assuring themselves that, after all, at the price I would be paying for it, it would still be a "great deal."

I feel sure, then, that after someone suggested giving me this other car, the dealer, in a weak moment, said, "Okay, fine. I'll take care of it. I don't think it really matters to him." Two days later, on a Monday, I had called him to ask when the car would be ready for me. "Did you look closely at it?" he asked. So I told him no, thinking that the car may have some small, inconsequential thing wrong with it, such as a nick or scratch.

When I went in later to pick up the car, my friend the dealer had told me that it was waiting downstairs and that the finance manager would take care of the papers for me. In retrospect, I remembered something odd: how all the various people in the dealership just kept looking at me in complete silence as I passed by them. Then I saw the car—which wasn't at all the one I had ordered. I could tell, too, from the serial number that this car had been in stock for some while, long before the other one was even manufactured.

I went back to see my friend the dealer. As I looked into his office, he seemed very busy, as he normally is, so I had to wait to see him. "Well, they switched cars on me," I told him finally. "That car has two thousand miles on it." I felt very embarrassed for him when I took him out and showed him the car. And you guessed it: I did not drive that car home, even though I knew that it too was a "good deal" for the money. What had been done was not nice at all, and it violated my trust in him and his whole organization.

Choosing a Dealership

What are some of the things to consider and look for in choosing a dealership?

WHO IS THE HUNGRIEST DEALER?

Look at the advertising of the dealers you are considering and try to determine which one seems the most eager to sell. He may offer a better deal than a more complacent seller.

Sometimes a downtown dealer will bend over backward to make a deal with you because clients don't want to drive a few extra miles to the inner city. The same could be true of any dealer located in an impoverished neighborhood, city, or state.

Then again, the hungriest dealer might be the one located closest to your home.

EARNED REPUTATIONS

The ways in which the dealer reaches the public are important. By paying attention to them, you can find out a lot.

Are the word-of-mouth comments you hear about this dealership uniformly positive, or nearly so?

Have you heard the dealer's radio advertisements, and, if so, are they informative as to his cars, services, and sales philosophy?

Does the print advertising seem informative, honest, and consistent?

If you live in an area in which local dealers advertise on TV, do you find these ads informative and carefully prepared, or just flashy and hyped up to get people to come into the place?

When there is a coupon or special offer, does the dealer really have the promised number of available cars and services or whatever else he has advertised? (Some dealers advertise a thousand cars to choose from. But most of these cars might have to be subsequently ordered from the factory and received over a period of time. You might only be able to see 150 to 200 cars.)

QUESTIONS RELATING TO THE PREMISES

When you walk into a dealership's domain, you can quickly determine how interested he is in his clients. If the facilities are comfortable and clean, he probably intends to give you service later. If they are not, it is fairly apparent that he doesn't care about maintaining any relationship with you in the future—which is a tipoff about the quality of his service department, for one thing. And followup service is a vital matter to many car buyers.

Make special note of the following observations:

- What is the overall appearance of the place, inside and out?
- Are the showroom, service center, and other rooms well lighted?
- Is this place of business clean and inviting, or dark, dingy, and disorderly looking?
- Is the restroom clean?
- Is there a customer lounge?
- What kind of employees are in the dealership? Are they friendly and courteous to both clients and each other? And are they attentive to their appearance?
- Does the sales staff show a pleasantly aggressive attitude?

(Let's hope so, for this shows a good, healthy atmosphere in which to conduct business. Avoid salespeople who exert high pressure yet are essentially indifferent toward clients.)

• Are there a good number of new cars on the premises so that you'll have plenty of models to look at and even drive?

• Does the dealership promise immediate or swift delivery on popular models of cars? Or would it take six or eight weeks to get the car you want?

VISIT THE SERVICE DEPARTMENT

Go into the service area as part of your tour. Meet the service manager, the parts manager, and the body shop manager. You may have to deal with them later on. Find out how willing they are to talk with you even when they don't feel obligated to. Of course they cannot afford to waste time in their busy schedules, but they should at least be courteous.

Ask any clients waiting there to tell you frankly about the quality of the service given to their cars. If they have any grievances, major or minor, you can expect to hear about them, sometimes even within earshot of employees. Try to filter out any petty or seemingly unjustifiable complaints.

You might even want to try out the service department on your present car before you buy a new one from the dealership. If you like the way they take care of a car they did not sell, you can be fairly certain to like how they handle one with their dealership's tag on it.

GO AND MEET THE DEALER HIMSELF

A good dealer—and by this I mean the head man at a dealership—should be available to you if you want to talk. Don't let him or someone else tell you he is always too busy.

If you want to see a dealer in person, go with or without an appointment and just ask to see him. It is a good sign if he is available; it indicates this dealer may have an open door policy.

When you ask to go in, don't tell anyone why you want to meet him. You should get the white glove treatment if you get right to the point and candidly say, "I just wanted to find out what kind of business you run, because I'm considering buying a car from you."

Please, however, respect the dealer's time. You may accidentally come in when the dealer or his surrogate has an appointment elsewhere or is closing an important deal.

If you do schedule a meeting with a dealer, show up, or else phone him if you find you can't make it. It's a matter of common courtesy.

As you talk with a dealer, try to discover his working philosophy. Does he want to serve people? Take care of his clients? If so, you probably can come directly to this dealer for help with future problems.

Some dealerships have absentee owners who might be involved in some field other than the auto business. So if you go in and ask for the dealer and they say, "He owns the dealership but usually isn't here; Mr. Smith runs the place," by all means ask to see Mr. Smith. If he comes out and shakes your hand and talks seriously to you, you've got a good sign.

A good dealer will consider you a friend if you point out any deficiencies or weaknesses in a helpful way. He will act grateful if you share with him major or even minor things that have bothered you or if you suggest ways in which services to clients might be improved.

If you work up courage and do tell some of these things to a dealer but find that he acts irritated or uninterested, beware! You are surely inside the wrong dealership. If you have already bought there, so much the worse. Instead of landing in a dealership that is truly concerned about improving itself, you apparently hit one that just wants the fast buck—with no more grief than necessary from the client.

Any dealership worth its salt has ongoing training and review or feedback programs for both sales and service staffs.

Other Things to Watch For in Dealerships

In small dealerships, the owners will probably make almost all decisions. The larger the unit is, the more likely then that department managers make most decisions concerning their own area (but according to company policy).

Whatever the dealership size, you should expect sufficient communication among those in charge so that you know you are dealing with a team of managers and support staff all pulling in the same direction. Key people must agree on policy matters and stand behind one another's word. If somebody tells you one thing but another person does not support it, that becomes their own internal problem, and shouldn't be yours to suffer.

The larger the dealership, the more important it will be for you to get all the sales arrangements, warranties, and other promises in writing.

Some department managers become so set in their ways that they do not accept suggestions from the owner-dealers or even from consultants called in by the dealers. By becoming so inflexible they may severely curtail their chances for advancement.

Whatever the circumstance, though, beware doing business with a dealership in which there appears to be a dispute or confusion in authority. True, you could make the disharmony or rivalry work somehow to your own benefit. But this situation ultimately works against the client, not for him.

Other types of dealerships to steer clear of until they get their problems settled:

• Any in which the manager obviously doesn't want to pay the price for developing a professional staff.

• A place where the manager is still learning and may be doing so at your expense.

• Any place in which the manager seems to be a person who may have been successful at something else (sales or mechanics, typically) but is just not the managerial sort.

Become a Professional Buyer

Within the ranks of professional salespeople there are the super pros, who exceed all others regardless of economic conditions, and the average salesmen, whose luck seems to go up and down with the times.

Generally speaking, successful car dealers began their apprentice period as car salesmen. They know the process involved in getting people to buy, and they try to hire and keep the best salesmen in their showrooms, backing them up with an outstanding service and parts department.

Counter this professionalism with your own. Take charge of the whole selling process when you go out to buy your car. Aim to become a professional buyer. You should go into the automobile dealership prepared to effectively counter the salesman. Don't be an easy mark for his skillful sales tactics.

Call Me When You Can

Flying Dan Donovan went into a Cadillac dealership. He told the salesman, "I want to buy a car today, and I want your best deal right now." The salesman said, "This is what it'll cost you." Dan said, "This is how much I will give you—" and he named a much lower figure. The salesman told him, "We can't sell it for that price." Dan then headed for the door, saying, "Fine, call me when you can."

A week later he got a phone call. The salesman asked, "You still want to buy that car?" "Yup, still do, and at *my* price." The salesman replied, "We can't sell it for that price. Would you buy it for this price?" and he gave a price some hundreds lower than before. However, Dan said, "Nope, sorry. Call me when you can sell it to me at my price."

Another week passed. And the salesman called again. "Mr. Donovan, do you still want to buy that car?" "I sure do—at my price," Dan answered. And the salesman said, "Come on down and pick it up."

Dan went into another dealership to buy a Japanese car. After several trips he was told the price was the best price; they wouldn't discount the car. "I live just up the street," Dan said. "What you're telling me is that I have to go elsewhere to buy the car." As he started out the door, the manager lowered the price by $1,700. Dan bought the car and drove it home.

Understanding the Current Car Market

A professional salesman understands the seller's market, where he functions easily and makes the best profits. In a seller's market, demand for the goods exceeds the supply, so that prices are usually high.

In a buyer's market, supply of goods exceeds the demand. Prices generally are low. Such markets usually stem from temporary economic conditions. It is under these adverse selling conditions that the crack salesman displays his greatest abilities.

As a professional buyer you should understand both the seller's market and the buyer's market. When you are about to buy a car you must know which market currently prevails—particularly concerning the kind of car you intend to buy. As I discussed in Chapter 5, you are likely to get a better deal from dealers selling American cars than from those handling popular foreign makes. Elitist cars tend to exist within a seller's market because they are in short supply with a comparatively high demand.

The market from 1979 to 1982 was mostly a buyer's market for domestic cars, because the supply had by far exceeded the demand at most dealerships.

The economic recovery of the last several years has revived sales of the American car and brought back—a bit tenuously, considering trade deficit problems in steel and the continuing popularity of foreign cars—a seller's market in automobiles. Of course, many good deals can still be made.

March 1985 saw an important development as President Reagan made a decision not to continue asking the Japanese to self-impose annual quotas of 1,850,000 Japanese-made cars exported to the United States. The Japanese responded with common sense, not flooding the U.S. with hundreds of thousands of additional cars, but continuing to provide at a steady pace their stripped-down, low-priced models. This strategy did not so much help the American consumer as position the Japanese to compete with the new Korean car—the Hyundai—about to enter the United States market in 1986, at a $5,000 to $7,000 sticker price.

The Japanese are now running from the sharp and aggressive Koreans with their cheap, high-quality cars, just as the United States automakers ran from the Japanese.

In 1984 the Koreans introduced their car into the Canadian market, hoping to sell 7,000 cars, and were pleasantly surprised to have sold 22,000. Thank Japan for high-quality cars; now, thank Korea for cheap, high-quality cars.

However, all this is not good news for the American worker or the trade deficit. The domestic automakers have really been concentrating on quality, and while making enormous progress *and* profit, the failure or success of the Saturn Project by General

Motors may still determine their future. Whatever happens, all of us should thank American car makers for their technological know-how, teamwork, dedication, determination, and courage in a crisis.

Awareness of changes in the economy, then, should be part of a professional buyer's considerations about when and how to buy.

How Dealers Use Advertising as a Come-On

Car advertising is like fishing: Once you come into a showroom or lot, they aim to sink a hook in you. Either you bite or they'll snag you, unless you are clever and adroit at eluding their tactics. The sport really begins as they try to land you. The whole process can take minutes, hours, days, weeks, months, or even years.

Some dealers spend a lot of money to get buyers into their showrooms. As part of their promotion they advertise huge tent sales, big discounts, and rebates. They may offer free bicycles, vacations, grills, or TV sets. They actually border on breaking Federal Trade Commission advertising regulations when they say something is free, when in effect its cost is really built into the price.

But somewhere you must pay for these things. Your emotions can get you involved so dramatically that you become a lay-down—an easy sale. And you wind up paying a price that is much higher than you would have paid otherwise, had you gone in for the cool and skillful bargaining that this book will teach you.

For example, a dealership advertised 6.9 percent interest on loans when the prime rate was 11.5, and then built the difference into the purchase price. Automatically the buyer paid a higher price for the car, lost additional income tax deductions, and was penalized by getting less of a return if he prepaid the loan.

When you read or hear dealers' hype, do keep firmly in mind that the only *special prices* are factory-sponsored, such as rebates, lowered prices, special assistance to all dealers of a brand franchise, special interest rate programs, and government-assisted programs. *Other than those, there are no special prices!*

Remember too that all dealers belonging to a franchise pay the same price for their cars. It is up to the individual dealer, therefore, to decide on the kind of deal he is willing to offer, or let his salesmen offer, to individual buyers and to the public.

The more a dealer cuts from the sticker price, the less profit the dealership is going to make. But increasing the sales volume can make up for decreased profit per sale. And in slow periods a few sales at diminished profits are much better than none. So watch for times when a dealership is looking to expand its sales volume (perhaps competing with a dealership across town) or when business is clearly dragging.

Unified Freight and a slow economy have put some car brokers across the country out of business. With Unified Freight every like car and model is charged the same regardless of destination. In other words, a dealership located in Los Angeles will be charged no more for freight than one located close to Detroit.

Consumers purchase new cars from franchised new car dealerships, not from the manufacturer. You might purchase a car through a car-buying service or broker, but they too buy from a dealer. You are better off buying directly from the dealer, where you can make your own deal.

A Few Words about Dealers

Dealerships are not owned by the manufacturers. Most dealers affiliate with a particular manufacturer and concentrate on sales and service of that make, but each dealer is an independent businessman.

Many people who make their living from car sales, however, are not familiar with the multitude of responsibilities in the business, including the need to show proper concern for the buying public.

In order to survive, an automobile dealer has to wear many hats. The complexity of operating a large dealership would rival that of many Fortune 500 companies.

A dealer must operate at least four businesses simultaneously: selling new cars, buying and reselling used cars, providing mechanical service, and supplying parts. Some also have additional businesses, such as body shops, vehicle leasing, truck sales, and finance insurance departments.

I could talk on and on about some of the great people in the automobile business. You may know a few right in your own town. What they all have in common is that they make things happen. They are movers and shakers.

Many dealers use their first dealerships as launching pads for investing wisely in more dealerships, real estate, or other related businesses until they become millionaires. The best dealers are the successful men who take care of their employees, are loyal to their customers, and give good service.

Now let's move on to the person at a dealership with whom you are likely to have the closest and most crucial contact: the salesman. He or she deserves a whole chapter of introduction so as to prepare you for the ultimate confrontation.

Step up to the best deal in town!

SEVEN

Let's Introduce the Salesman

Carolina's Tryout Terry drove to Greenville to look at the new cars—his favorite pastime. Pappy Davis greeted him and soon had him out driving a car he liked.

When they pulled into the showroom, Tryout Terry said, "Thanks, I'll see you around." Somehow, though, Pappy adroitly waltzed him into the closing office and gently put pressure on him to buy *now*. Tryout Terry kept trying to inch away.

But Pappy sensed that he had really *liked* that car. So he said, "We've got a customer coming in this afternoon who's looking for a used car just like yours. If we can get a big bundle for it, wouldn't you want to use it as a trade-in that would cover the down payment?"

Tryout Terry took the bait. He drove that new car home with him, and as soon as he pulled in the driveway his kids squealed, "Hey, Mom, we got a new car!" Uncle Lyman and Aunt Norie stood around beaming. And three neighbors came by, each commenting, "What a beaut that Shazam is, Terry." . . . "Must be swell to have money like that!" . . . "Boy, I do wish I could get me a purple one."

All Tryout Terry did was expand his chest and smile. Once he took the demo home, he just couldn't bring himself to say, "But it's not *mine*. I'm only trying it out to see how I like it."

He didn't smile much when Pappy told him the next day, after he brought the car back, that they hadn't gotten the high offer they had expected on Terry's own car. Terry, though disappointed, used it as a trade-in anyhow—though he had to add some hundreds of dollars more as additional down payment.

Tryout Terry was stuck. Because he had jumped at Pappy's invitation to let him take the car home to show his family, he committed himself before he was really ready to. And he hadn't had the chance to shop around, either to get his new car at a lower price or to sell his trade-in at a higher one.

Next time maybe he'll think twice before responding to a salesman's generous offer to let him take a joy ride in a demo.

Understanding Salesmen

Knowing something about how salesmen operate will help you when you go out to buy your next car. If you are acquainted with their basic tactics and psychology, it will be easier to determine what your plan of action and your response to them should be.

Nothing—or almost nothing—salesmen say should sway you from your own good judgment and particular interests and needs. Be prepared for their blandishments. Your own determined behavior could gain their respect and work to your advantage.

You may know quite a bit about sales and marketing techniques already. Maybe you do some selling yourself. But don't assume that you know everything you need to know about the car salesman. Unless you're in the business yourself, you won't be wholly prepared for what happens. Car selling is a special field, and the car salesman's universally acknowledged reputation for hard and slick selling is justifiably earned. He is trained to tell you the things you want to hear, to be a good listener, to ask questions, and to answer your questions with questions. He will always sell to your emotions and senses: sight, smell, touch, sound, and taste.

This highly trained guided missile can take your wallet out of your britches while he's smiling at you—and make you like it.

How Salesmen Operate

Salesmen are the cogs that keep a dealership going. Each employee is vital to the success of the business. You should learn, and even come to appreciate, how they are trained to get you to relax and feel comfortable, to be able to control and convince you. If you understand this before going into a dealership, *you* can take control rather than forfeiting it to the salesman.

A salesman learns on the job. In reality, almost *no* funds are spent to train salesmen, compared to the millions of dollars spent by the auto industry on advertising and billions of dollars spent on research and development.

Through the years the salesman has been variously called merchant, trader, storekeeper, solicitor, peddler, hawker, drummer, hustler, huckster, middleman, confidence or "con" man, and many other things—some of them unprintable. Sales, after all, have made the world of commerce go round for thousands of years.

Salesmen should have a strong natural grasp of marketing, merchandising, and psychology. In past centuries, salesmen were either "born to the trade" or acquired skills on their feet, in practice. Nowadays there are thousands of special training seminars and institutes that can produce effective salespeople. Colleges and universities have business administration departments that feature preparatory courses for future sellers and programs that update the skills of working professionals.

A key ingredient in any salesman's success is the infusion of positive thinking and enthusiasm. These elements can be communicated to customers so that they suddenly have the urge to buy.

It's particularly important for you to understand the high-powered salesman, the superstar seller. A dealership really needs him, not only to boost sales but to serve as a model for less inspired salespeople. It might just be your fate—and in fact good fortune if you're able to control the proceedings yourself—to have one attach himself to you when you walk in a showroom.

He will be among the 20 percent of salesmen who sell 80 percent of the cars. Watch and admire his tactics, his charm, his cleverness, but don't let him budge you from your plan.

The salesman knows he must be likable and entertaining while being earnest and convincing. But no matter how favorably a customer responds to a salesman's personality and persuasiveness, he or she should not lose track of the fact that this person's mission in life is to sell.

Selling Charm along with Cars

In almost all walks of life men and women are constantly selling not only products, but *themselves* too.

As with a newly dating couple, in a sales situation the aura of romance, charm, and desirability may pervade the scene. The sheer dynamics of coming to terms, of gaining or relinquishing control, often make the air in a showroom tingle with overtones that are nearly sexual.

Quite seriously, you should be wary of this chemistry, in both yourself and the salesperson opposite you, who is attuned to wooing you in a variety of ways. The special psychology of sexual attraction enables a salesperson to manipulate buyers who are obviously vulnerable to this form of hypnotic or physiological persuasion.

Women buyers are particularly vulnerable, not only because they tend to be less knowledgeable about cars and less sure of themselves when bargaining, but also because most salespeople are men. I would have to say that a large percentage of men everywhere are perpetually "on the make." Car salesmen are no exception.

Many women, young or middle-aged, looking for a date or a new boyfriend, or trying to find out if they are still attractive to men (perhaps besides their husband), might be swayed by a car salesman's charisma and seeming sincerity. They will end up buying something they might not otherwise have bought, or will pay far more than they should.

So I am suggesting that if a woman is searching for romance, a car showroom is not the wisest place to find it! Especially when she risks losing thousands of dollars by naively falling for a salesman's seductive selling charm.

Only a small percentage of car salespeople are women. This lamentable inequity is rooted not in job discrimination but in the age-old distractions and complications of heterosexual chemistry. Dealers have found that a great deal of time and energy can get wasted on idle play. A well-run dealership that keeps its salespeople busy can avoid much of this.

Women who succeed in the retail car business are disciplined, strong-willed, clear-thinking professionals. Some of them are salespeople; others are sales managers, general managers, and dealers. There should be more of them! Many women, of course, work as managers or support staff in all departments, but primarily the office.

Basic Salesmen's Characteristics

It won't be too difficult for you to tell the difference between a good salesman (sharp and skillful) and a bad one (inept or indifferent). Of greater concern is the dishonest salesman, whose slick techniques are harder to detect. Watch for indicators of unethical conduct that are holdovers from the bad old days of car selling (and that supposedly still infect the used car market in some places. I'll tell some tales later on).

Let's consider some salient features in salesmen.

Salesmen must like talking to people, both in person and on the telephone. They should be organized and follow a plan in order to make their efforts more effective.

Salesmen are trained to look people straight in the eye. They understand that this generates a feeling of trust.

Salesmen have received training from peers, supervisors, dealers, and consultants on how to interact with customers. Therefore, what the customer deals with much of the time is not the natural personality of the salesman himself, but a composite that has been brought about to enhance his sales potential.

Salesmen should be clean and neat. Dress codes vary, depending on geographical location and dealer preference. Generally speaking, the dealer sets the standard with his own attire. This also includes length of hair, type of haircut, and acceptance or rejection of facial hair.

The salesman has to learn to "read people," to comprehend body language—both his and his customers'—and to "read between the lines" of what others say.

In the Showroom

A salesman also has to know how to approach and understand customers, to anticipate their needs and interests and to alleviate their anxieties. This can't be accomplished by repeating the same set speech to each person who comes in. If you get one who talks as if by rote, you'll know that you have met inexperience, unsureness, or boredom. The first two you might be willing to cope with, especially if you sense that by getting the upper hand in negotiating you can work things your way. But you should shake away a bored salesman at once; he won't merit the sales commission he might get from your purchase.

The salesman's purpose should be to help customers buy. Salesmen know that most customers have not purchased a new or used car for two to five years. It may shock a customer to realize how much prices have risen since he or she last looked at cars. This is called sticker shock. In recent years customers have experienced it more than ever before.

The salesman may walk the line with you while you look at different cars. Even though you may already have expressed a definite choice, he will try to tell you about every model the dealership carries and assure you that something they have will suit you wonderfully well. He takes time for this show because some customers are impulse buyers. But this is also a sign of his own professionalism.

Do you doubt me? I have had the experience of talking to people who came in saying something like, "We must have a two-door sedan. It must be blue. It has to be a standard shift, not automatic. And it must not cost over X number of dollars." Yet this same party would afterward purchase a brown four-door station wagon with automatic transmission and pay 50 percent more than the maximum price that had been stated!

Early in the negotiation, a sales pro determines what type of buyer you are: a cash buyer, payment buyer, difference buyer (who wants to know how much money—difference—he has to pay between his trade-in and new car), trade allowance buyer, discount buyer, or "can you get me financed" buyer. Even if you aren't buying that day, a professional salesman will always give you his time, never trying to qualify you as "flaky" or a "turkey."

A shrewd salesman will not tell you that the dealership does not have the car you want in stock. This is because at that very moment the car could be coming off the transport truck. Or the dealer may have just traded for the exact car, or almost the exact car, you want. (And if he hasn't, he usually can do so swiftly, to get the car you're after, especially if he's located in a large metropolitan area.)

*You said you were going to train me. . . . Go get 'em pal—you're
ready. . . .*

A successful salesman must have charisma. He must be able to say things that other people cannot say, things that will convince customers to trust him. For example, he will steer the customer away from certain cars, saying such things as, "No, I've heard that one is accident-prone." . . . "To be honest with you, that car isn't a very good buy for the money." You'll inevitably appreciate his concern for you and his sensitivity to the kind of car you should have.

How Salesmen Are Paid

Good salesmen can earn $24,000 to $70,000 annually, depending on how they are motivated, where they work, and what the pay plan is. Some salesmen earn more, but they are the exceptional super-stars. (Sales commissions are generally $100 to $150 on most ordinary cars, but can go up to $1,000 or $1,500 on luxury cars.)

Some salesmen believe in saying outright, "I'm a salesman. I'm paid a salary. Management keeps track of what I sell and get paid, and whether I sell you a car or not. So I'll make you a good deal on a car." Others take a different approach, the gist of which might be: "I'm a salesman. I work on commission, and if I don't sell a car, I don't get paid. You're one of the most important people on the face of the earth to me today. So I'll give you a good deal . . . or I'll give you a great trade-in allowance."

A Supersalesman in Action

In this era of gimmicks and giveaways, salesmanship is looked upon as either meaningless or a lost art. In one dealership in Atlanta, a salesman is proving with amazing results that good salesmanship still sells more cars than free TV sets can.

The salesman is Todd. How does he do it? First, he learned that in order to be successful, he has to have many satisfied customers—and the more the better. He talks to them when they come in and bends over backward to be fair and decent with them.

The result? They buy cars. He does say, though, that one big reason for any individual's success is the dealer's policies.

Here is an analysis of his sales techniques:

- He knows his cars well, provides good answers to all questions and counters objections with practical reasoning.
- He refuses some sales—realizing that customers are going beyond their financial capabilities.
- He believes in second demonstrations when the customer appears uncertain.
- He does not bad-mouth competitors or their cars.
- He sells with the idea that each customer must be so satisfied with the deal that he or she will send in at least two other customers.

Let me expand now upon these points.

Todd calls for knowing more than just product specifications. He studies all pertinent figures so that he doesn't have to interrupt a sales pitch to look them up. He also anticipates objections, proving that what the customer may consider a disadvantage is actually beneficial.

A salesman never likes to say no. A car salesman is taught to sell to anybody and everybody and to let the financial institutions decide who can and cannot afford the payments. But Todd considers the referrals he gets, so when he sees that a customer is not in a position to assume financial debt, he advises him to wait a few months until his present car is paid off, other debts are out of the way, or his basic income improves. These people come back later and thank him for delaying them—and they buy, too. Ultimately Todd's forthrightness pays off in added sales. People trust him and freely recommend him to their friends.

When Todd sees that a customer is wavering, he concentrates on getting him into the car and letting him drive it himself—while Todd sits beside him and points out performance and ease of handling. Such prospects need verification that their judgment is good. The second demonstration gives them confidence.

Many customers have had bad experiences with other dealers and will make baited remarks or ask leading questions. Todd has a policy of not rising to the bait. He'll also admit that competitive makes are excellent and that other dealers have been successful. He focuses on himself, praising his own cars and the advantages of doing business with him. He never makes snide remarks about his competition. By keeping this principle, he feels he wins the customer's respect and confidence.

Todd, like all good salesmen, sells with referrals in the back of his mind. Referred customers already want to buy and trust the salesman because he was recommended by a friend. First of all, Todd deals fairly and honestly with each and every customer, because someone who becomes unhappy with a deal will not refer friends to him. Second, Todd asks them to send their friends to him. And third, after the sale he sends a letter to each customer, offering to help whenever necessary and again asking the person to send in any friends who are thinking of buying a car.

Watch Out for the Unethical Salesman

Unfortunately, not all car salesmen observe the Golden Rule. Most are well-meaning but still fall short of Todd's standards. And some are downright unprincipled in their dealings with customers. You could really lose some money.

Would you believe it? In the bad old days, a salesman might throw a customer's car keys onto the roof of the nearest building, or in some other way manage to lose them after supposedly checking over the car for its trade-in value. Unless a customer happened to have an extra set of keys with him, he had no choice but to drive home the car that he was considering buying, or another one being demonstrated. The salesman was gambling that the customer would finally decide to buy the car—which often happened, of course, after the wife and kids saw it. This practice also prevented the customer from going to other dealerships to shop for other cars, or to get a complete quotation. This psychological maneuver conditions clients for "I will" and "I do" answers.

Car salesmen were scarcely known for their subtlety in devious dealings. Unethical salesmen might have unsuspecting customers sign a piece of paper before they went on a test drive. The signature was supposedly just for the dealership's records, with the salesman explaining to the customer, "This tells us that you have the car—enjoy it!" The customer, thinking he was just taking a test drive, returned to the dealership, only to find out that what he had signed was a finance contract, with the first payment due in thirty days.

Another trick was to tell a customer that he could not afford to pass up the low, low payments the dealership was offering—of only $69. Then when the payment book arrived, the amount due turned out to be $138. The perturbed buyer phoned his salesman and was told that $69 was the biweekly payment.

Sometimes a naive buyer was told by a salesman that the radio was in the trunk—and it turned out to be a $12.99 transistor. Or that the dealership would put a V-8 engine in the six-cylinder car when it was brought in for the thousand-mile inspection. Or that at some distant time an automatic transmission would be installed in their standard transmission car, or a radio, power steering, power brakes, air conditioner, heater—whatever was missing that the customer most desired. But of course when it came time for reckoning, the buyer would discover that the understanding had been oral: There was nothing on paper to prove such pie-in-the-sky promises.

Strange underhanded financial dealings might go on behind customers' backs. For instance, one unscrupulous salesman had a gambling habit. To cover his debts he eventually financed twenty-five cars sold to customers who had paid cash. On each transaction he used much of the cash in an attempt to win back losses. And all the while he was making multiple car payments. Finally, when the salesman couldn't cover one of the payments, the bank sent a late payment notice to the car owner. The customer informed the bank that a mistake was made because he had paid cash. An investigation began, and the salesman soon took up residence in Michigan's "Big Top"—Jackson State Prison.

Another unethical sales tactic that has prevailed for many years is "bait and switch." An ad announces an incredibly low price for a particular car. But somehow the car is already sold or out of stock when you arrive to buy it. Then the salesman tries to sell you something other than the advertised special. This game is by no means confined to the retail auto business.

Another form of bait and switch can be even more annoying. A salesman takes an order from a customer for a particular car, only to turn around and sell the car to another customer who offered him a better deal. (This practice has soured a number of buyers on a particular manufacturer, dealership, or dealer—who are rarely responsible themselves for the outcome.)

One more practice that dates back to the bad old days is advertising very low-priced loss leaders, or a one-of-a-kind stripped-down car, in order to get customers to come and visit the

Hey, I thought my payments were $69.00 a month.

dealership. The salesmen were then responsible for getting the customers to buy one of the higher-priced selections. Sometimes salesmen were given a little extra negative motivation: The dealer, or manager, threatened that any salesman who actually *sold* the come-on car was going with it—out the door.

It is certainly true that some trusting, unsuspicious people have been hurt over the years. In time, however, such nasty tricks boomerang. The dealership suffers as word spreads of its unethical tactics. Therefore most dealers nowadays work hard to uphold their business reputation by not hiring salespeople who appear to lack principles, firmly instilling an ethical code in their employees, and dismissing at once anybody who has dealt in an underhanded way with a customer.

And Spot the Drifters

In some places—California for some reason especially—there is a trend for salesmen to float from dealership to dealership. Quality dealerships simply avoid hiring these drifters.

The dealer who takes on salesmen who are just floating through will soon have a lot of problems on his hands. These drifters also alienate the rest of the sales force because of their independence, their cynicism, and their bad habits.

Remember always that the fast deal is by no means always the best deal. The drifter is a fast-deal expert. A drifter is generally not around to help the customer with any later problems that may develop. If you visit a dealership that has a lot of obvious drifters on its staff, watch out. Often they are interested only in selling you a car today. They couldn't care less about your problems tomorrow.

How can you spot a drifter? He usually has a broad, toothy smile and gives you a long-lost-buddy back pat. And he also might have a way of glancing sideways—doubtless watching out for the sheriff or bill collector who often is dogging his heels.

Another bad apple is the salesman who moonlights or "curbs" cars. He buys a customer's car personally and sells it outside the dealership. If a salesman or manager gives you anything other than a dealership check when purchasing your car, tell the dealer. Likewise, when buying, tell the dealer if you are asked to write a check to anyone other than the dealership.

Promises, Promises

Promises, promises . . . are what some salesmen use to keep customers from comparison shopping. Commonly, this type of unethical salesman strings you along by leading you to believe that you can buy at a very low price. The sales pitch might sound like this:

"Look, I am going to write up your offer, as ridiculously low as it is. I know the sales manager will not accept your offer right now. But okay these figures, sign your name by the X, and give me a solid deposit of a thousand dollars to show your good faith. I'll try to catch the sales manager in a good mood or when he is desperate to make extra sales and discuss it with him. Or I might try to present your deal at the same time I present a more solid deal."

Now the mood is set for the "bump." (The amazing thing is that you will raise your offer yourself. After all, the salesman has already told you that your offer was too low.) You call the salesman back later the same day or the next day to find out if there has been action on your offer. The answer invariably is, "The manager doesn't seem willing to accept your low offer. I need more time. Perhaps later today or tomorrow I'll be able to catch him at a weak moment."

The thought is now planted in your mind that if the offer had been good, they would have accepted it. The next thing the salesman will suggest is, "Why don't you let me see if I can't get the deal accepted with another twenty-five dollars?". . .or $50, $100, $500, or $1,000.

Another unethical but prevalent practice is the "low ball"— quoting an extremely attractive price to the customer, lower than it's at all possible to purchase a car for, in order to have the customer come back before buying anywhere else. Offers from other dealerships will thus sound too high during comparison shopping.

A salesman will "high ball" the customer by offering him a trade-in price higher than can be reasonably given. This way the customer will return, ready to make a deal.

A "bush" is agreeing on a dollar amount for the sale of the car. But when the customer comes to pick up the car, the salesman says, "I made a mistake. I can't deliver the car for that price. This is what you'll have to pay. . . ."

Then the negotiating starts again. The smart car buyer should get his deposit back and walk out, unless he is completely satisfied that the salesman made a legitimate mistake.

An unethical manager could put on quite a show for the customer and swear up and down that he is going to take the sale away from the offending salesman, or even that the salesman will be fired because of the mistake. Don't believe it. Such sales managers can be good actors.

One way to keep this from happening is to make certain the initial deal has been accepted *in writing* by the dealer or the dealership's sales manager. Then "mistakes" such as this will be much less likely to occur—especially in states, like Wisconsin, that have laws against such practices.

Other Ways Dealers Get Cars Sold

In an effective dealership campaign customers are offered a guaranteed trade-in price (usually around $700) for any vehicle they can drive to the lot, regardless of age or condition. Since the guaranteed trade-in amount is based on the dealer selling at the suggested retail price, a customer might bring in a totally worthless vehicle and the dealer could still make a decent profit. But the dealer's hot-selling or low-gross-profit models are likely to be excluded, since he may not make enough on them at such a sale to justify letting them go for promotional purposes.

Invariably during this type of promotion, customers bring in trade-ins worth more than the guaranteed amount. For some reason this campaign always draws a lot of customers with the ability to buy. They bring in their second (work or transportation) car to take advantage of the sale.

Dealers have an opportunity to practically steal customers' trade-ins by appraising them for much less than they could get elsewhere. Customers can get caught up in the hype of this promotion and lose all sense of direction.

Of course it doesn't do any harm to go, participate, and look around. But stay calm! No matter what the occasion, stick to your original plan.

And Then There's Just Bad Salesmanship

I'll never forget Joe from my early years as a car salesman. Joe didn't care about the cars he was selling, one way or the other. But he would sell any and every car—and fast!

These were the days when the Corvair was first being introduced. After the sales staff at Shalla Chevrolet had finished studying the new material on the Corvair, they were given an oral quiz. The first prize (which I ended up winning) was a $100 savings bond. It was an incentive for the salesmen to study and learn about the product they were going to sell.

Joe wasn't interested in any $100 bonds if they required some studying. He was eager to sell cars on commission—and to do it rapidly. The first question someone asked Joe was, "Of what metal is the new Corvair engine made?" Joe's answer was, "Holy Cheez, how should I know? Alum-ahnum-ahnum-ahnum. All I gonna ask the customer is: 'You wanna engine inna front or inna back?' "

(For those readers unfamiliar with the Corvair, the air-cooled engine is in the rear compartment. The Corvair is heated with a gas heater in the front compartment.)

Joe's first customer at the new car showing was an elderly woman. This gracious, well-groomed lady wanted to see the engine of the marvelous offering, the Corvair. Joe politely opened the hood. The lady asked, "But where is the engine?" Joe pointed to the gas heater. The lady commented that it seemed to be awfully small. Joe stood up straight and said, "Yes, madam, this is an economy car."

Hearing this, I excused myself from the customer I was assisting. I stepped over and told the lady, "Joe was explaining the economy of the gas heater and now wants to show you the all-new air-cooled anodized aluminum engine."

Joe smiled and said, "Thank you, Mr. Page. . . . Now, madam, I would like you to inspect the car engine." Opening the back compartment, he asked, "Isn't it beautiful?" The lady purchased the car.

Product knowledge is important in serving customers properly. It was fitting that when a salesman drove his air-cooled Corvair into the service department and asked to have the antifreeze checked in a car that did not use water, the mechanics jokingly charged him $12!

Then there's the ho-hum salesman, Motormouth, who just loves to talk. He has to tell you absolutely everything and continues to pass up chances for closing the deal, despite the fact that you are clearly ready to sign and get on with other business.

If you do run into a situation in which you practically have to lead the salesman into making his own sale, I doubt that he is anywhere near to becoming a professional. If a salesman does not learn to close a sale, he may watch "hot" customers—those ready for a sale—walk out on him, and learn later that they bought a car at the next dealership they went to.

But suppose you stay with Motormouth in your determination to get a car. If he continues to drag, just say, "How soon can I have my car?" If such a direct question does not stir the salesman into action—to have you sign and put up your deposit—until he is through with his story, you have a really incompetent, boring, failure-prone dolt on your hands.

If you do stick it out with the sales dunce but continue to be dissatisfied with the way he handles the transaction, go ahead and finish up. But later tell the dealer how badly the sale was handled. By alerting him to the salesmen's incompetence, you will be helping him run a better business.

Don't expect to have such a problem, however. Most dealers cannot afford to keep someone on staff or on a commission basis who does not consistently bring good profits into the organization. An indolent or indifferent car salesman is almost a contradiction in terms!

And now let's move on to the showroom itself, where most of the action is.

NOTES:

Anything you want . . . we'll make your dreams come true!

EIGHT

The Trip to the Showroom

Happy Harold, Georgia's jolly sales pro, constantly looked for facial expressions, good or bad, and listened for buzzwords from prospects as he showed them cars.

One day, as he was explaining a car's features to Lippy Lizzie, he watched for that first smile and then waited to hear those special expressions: "I love the sleek lines," "The interior is just beautiful," "I feel so safe in here."

Lizzie had come to the showroom only out of curiosity, really, to see the line of new cars. She wasn't ready to *buy* one. But Happy Harold picked up on her buzzwords and repeated them over and over in new and different forms, like an incantation.

Smiling and talking, Harold hypnotized Lizzie into signing for that new car she didn't really need.

Are you ready for your first trip to dealerships that interest you?

Yes, you have done that all-important investigative work beforehand and made up your car-shopping list. And you have given thought to how you'll act when you come face to face with the salesman in his own territory.

As almost all of us know, however, real encounters can go very differently indeed from the way we anticipated. So anyone who feels at all unsure should do some practicing.

Before you meet the salesman, be absolutely certain that you are well prepared to withstand the selling campaign that will begin with your arrival.

Rehearse for Your Role as Car Buyer

If you are uncertain about dealing directly with a car salesman, particularly if you have never bought a car before, you would do well to spend extra time preparing yourself for this encounter. I recommend that you try some private role-playing to gain ease and expertise in handling the kind of approach and dialogue required to hold your own. Maybe you'll even gain control of the bargaining.

Resolve to go after what you want and *only* what you want, to stay in command even if you have to use written reminders.

Read the next section on "Seven Sets of Seven Magic Words." Then commit these sentences—or something very much like them, in words that come naturally to you—to memory.

Look over your professional checklist again. Argue with yourself about your choices. Then play the part of a salesman who tries to talk you into options you don't need or can't afford. Resuming your own identity, stand firm with this imaginary salesman and all his cajoling.

Have all these arguments down pat *before* you go in to confront the real people at the dealerships you chose. Rehearse before a mirror if it helps. Change roles as many times as necessary to reinforce your ability to stick to your checklist. (Obviously, unless you have forewarned others in your house it might be well to do this in private, lest you be put away.)

After you have argued with yourself until you are sure you can stay in command and stick to your plan, ask a friend or relative to test you. See if she or he can get you off the track. Have him give you a really hard sell. If he weakens your resolve, go back to the mirror. And practice some more.

Look in the mirror to perfect your eye-to-eye contact and your facial expressions. When saying the series of seven magic words, say them out loud to your mirror image. Use a tape recorder, if you have one. When you are happy with what you see and hear, practice seven more times.

When you feel fully confident, you are ready to go in automobile dealership and conquer the showroom.

Remember that the secret in negotiating is always to have control. If you're negotiating for a car, a home, or anything else, don't be afraid. Speak up. You never know what can be accomplished unless and until you try. And the only way you can try is by going out and doing it!

Seven Sets of Seven Magic Words

Would you like to have a simple method to buy a car and save money? You don't have to go to school or attend seminars in order to put it into effective operation. To assume control of the situation when you visit a dealership, confine your remarks on the car-buying transaction to the following seven sentences. If you want to restyle the wording to suit your own way of talking, that's okay, so long as you preserve the meaning.

So here are the Seven Sets of Seven Magic Words:

1. "I want to buy a car today."
2. "I don't want you to lose money."
3. "I want your best deal right now."
4. "Let's see how that looks on paper."
5. "How much trade-in allowance for my car?"
6. "Thank you for being my professional consultant."
7. "I like doing business with professional people."

As for the Seven Sets of Seven Magic Words: go ahead and mix them up in your own combinations. In fact, you may have to repeat some of the phrases over and over—especially the first three sets.

If you are considering a trade-in, regardless of how hard a salesperson presses you about the car you're driving, don't mention number 5. Just say, "I'm here to buy a car and don't have a trade-in to discuss." Leave your options open: you may sell the car on your own, as two-thirds of the people do; give it to a relative; or keep it for a second car. Later on, of course, you may actually decide that you want to trade it in. But don't mention number 5 until the appropriate time—after you've gotten the best deal on the car you want.

If you are timid, forget things, or have a physical affliction that affects your ability to speak, you can communicate with flashcards. You might write each set of Seven Magic Words on separate 3″ × 5″ cards, numbering them one through seven. Show the cards in sequence to the salesperson and smile (but not a toothy grin like the cat who just ate the canary).

These words will help put you in control. Practice them and try to get a feel for the right time to utter the next set. Timing is all-important. The first five sets especially take practice in assertiveness and timing. The final two sets are simply common courtesy. They show your appreciation for a professional attitude.

Now Try Them in the Showroom on a Real Salesman

"I WANT TO BUY A CAR TODAY"

With your shoulders back and a smile on your face, sound your battle cry firmly: "I want to buy a car today." Let it ring loud and clear. It isn't likely that you'll conclude a deal all in one day, of course, but telling the salesperson "I want to buy a car today" signals your willingness to purchase immediately if the right arrangement can be made.

Extend your hand to the salesman. Introduce yourself. Tell him that you want to be helped and what you are looking for. Give him a copy of the checklist you have prepared.

After you have made your announcement, "I want to buy a car today," and have made the few other remarks suggested here, stop talking and listen. Let the marketing pro do the talking. Even a few moments of silence on your part may seem like forever to you, but outlast them. They'll pay off in dollars.

If the salesman is a real pro, he will try to get full sticker price. In some cases this may be necessary because the markup is not that great on a small, low-priced car. However, the amateur salesman might say, "I'll take off one or two hundred dollars." Just smile while tossing your head back and comment, "Aw, come on!" Then keep quiet again, and don't break the silence.

(When you practice this in front of a mirror, keep at it until it seems natural to you. Always smile. Never be mean or degrading. Honey really does catch more flies than vinegar.)

Don't discuss your trade-in yet. Right now you are *buying* a car.

Remember to say "Aw, come on!" two or three times. Your crushing blow could be, "I told you, I want to buy a car today." Again, be silent and smile. Wait. Wait. Wait. The marketing pro may get up and leave to talk with a manager or bring a third party into the deal-making.

"I DON'T WANT YOU TO LOSE MONEY"

The conversation may go like this. The salesman says, "You're a smart buyer. Did you read Gordon Page's book about how to buy a car? What are you trying to do to us? We *have* to make a profit—Gordon told you this in his book. What will you offer us for the car?"

Your answer is: "I don't want you to lose money, but I'm going to buy a car today." Then shut up and smile some more.

You should be getting pretty good at this and by now should feel very comfortable. When they respond, and only if a third party has gotten involved, again say with a smile, "Aw, come on." And then more silence.

This can go on for an hour or hours if you allow it. Be patient. What else can they do when they have that one live bird in their hands, not several somewhere out there in the bush?

"I WANT YOUR BEST DEAL RIGHT NOW"

When you feel that neither the salesman, sales manager, nor dealer can or will go any further or if you have to leave, put the cake in the oven by saying again with a smile, but not laughingly, "I told you I'm going to buy a car today." Then add, "I want your best deal right now." These now become the seven most important magic words. They affirm your position of authority.

They will beg you to talk! But again, don't you dare break the silence. Whoever breaks the silence in this kind of wheeling and dealing loses.

"LET'S SEE HOW THAT LOOKS ON PAPER"

If they finally come up with a bid that sounds good to you, say the fourth set of seven magic words: "Let's see how that looks on paper." Be sure every detail about the deal is written down exactly as you agreed. Nothing you regarded as "included" should turn out to be "extra" when you read the fine print. Refer to your checklist to be sure that all the points are covered in the written agreement.

"HOW MUCH TRADE-IN ALLOWANCE FOR MY CAR?"

When the paperwork is done, say the fifth set of seven magic words: "How much trade-in allowance for my car?"

If you prepared properly, you have a fair idea of your car's wholesale (not retail) value. (It allows for the dealer's profit. He has to make a profit, after all, or he can't afford to stay in business.) A dealer's profit philosophy is that a good deal is sticker price while a great deal is over sticker.

Be sure the trade-in allowance is subtracted from the previously agreed-upon sale figure. You might get a puzzled or dirty look, but just smile. Remember, you have just made the best deal on the car you are purchasing.

"THANK YOU FOR BEING MY PROFESSIONAL CONSULTANT"

Don't forget to thank your salesman for his help in the transaction. After the sale is completed and again after the delivery, say the sixth set of seven magic words: "Thank you for being my professional consultant."

If you have followed directions up to here, you will not have let the salesman manage you at all—you will have kept control. Therefore, the salesman will be glad to be recognized as a professional consultant to a customer who knew how to get the best deal on the car he wanted—who has truly proved to be a professional buyer.

"I LIKE DOING BUSINESS WITH PROFESSIONAL PEOPLE"

This last set of seven magic words is a parting compliment to the salesman, the sales manager, and the dealer. After you say, "I like doing business with professional people," they are left with a good feeling about you, even though you have driven a harder bargain than many of their other customers. The deal you struck with them has given them less profit, but they'll respect you. It's a rare professional who does not actually enjoy a good bargaining fight.

Meeting a Salesman in a Showroom

If a good salesman hears that you are thinking about a new car, he begins doing his work by calling you and then inviting you to the dealership. Rather than being annoyed by his intrusiveness, you might feel fortunate to be in good hands. Following up a lead given to a salesman by a friend or acquaintance is part of his professional responsibility.

If you feel comfortable in your first encounter with a salesman, you could talk with him casually to find out more about him.

- Has he been around a good while? This indicates, of course, his steadiness on the job and the fact that he must be regarded as a valued employee.
- Is he going to be there to help you, not only before buying the car but also during the sale—and afterward, if you need him for any reason?
- Is this salesman someone to whom you would send a friend who wants to buy a car? (If not, be very reluctant to deal with him yourself!)

What to Expect from the First Meeting

When you walk into the showroom, a salesman should greet you immediately. He will introduce himself and then ask you, or expect to hear, your name as well. Don't be offended when he asks you, "What kind of car may I help you buy?" or some similar question. This is a sign of professionalism.

A pro will not say simply "Can I help you?" He knows that you wouldn't be there if you didn't want help of some kind. He might say, "What kind of car are you interested in looking at?" As the well-prepared customer, you should follow his greeting and say, "I would like to see . . ." and then tell him the kind of car that interests you in terms of size and style and price range.

The groundwork is set. Those first ten seconds in the sales encounter are crucial, for they make or break the connection between you and the salesman. As you feel each other out, he will be gathering information about you, the kind of car you are looking for, your financial status, and your present automobile. He can size you up in an informal way, so that you may hardly be aware of relaying vital information.

For example, Lance, Boston's supersalesman, asked a customer in a joking way, "You're in the Car-of-the-Month Club, aren't you? How much are your payments?" The customer relaxed and said, "Well, my payments are two hundred and thirty-five dollars a month." Lance then asked, "How many do you have left?" "Twenty," the customer replied. So, by multiplying twenty by $235, Lance knew his customer owed $4,700 on that car. Immediately, Lance had received some information in an easy and unobtrusive manner.

The following qualifying points will be covered in a relaxed manner by Lance:

• Size of the car you want
• Price range
• Type of equipment
• Is this the only dealership you've visited?
• If not, what other makes of cars have you seen? And what are your impressions of them?
• How do you plan to pay for the new car?
• How much do you have for a down payment?
• How much have you budgeted for car payments?
• Will your spouse want to see any car you're interested in?
• Will there be a trade-in?
• Is the trade-in fully paid for?
• If so, do you have the title with you?
• If not, how much is owed?
• And what are the payments?
• Where is it financed?
• Whose name is on the title?
• How long have you owned the trade-in?
• Why are you trading?
• How soon are you going to buy?
• Where do you work and how long have you been there?
• Where does your spouse work—and for how long?

The financial institution decides if you are a good or bad credit risk, not the dealer. The dealer, however, may venture an opinion. For example, the dealer may report that "He looks clean-cut, sounds like a good worker, and seems to have his act together."

Some people have appeared creditworthy to a dealer, even though they'd been turned town for financing. After being sent to a financial institution for a personal meeting, they've been given the loan.

Then He'll Show You Around

The salesman will ask the same questions about the car you want that you asked yourself when you made out your plan and checklist.

Save everyone's time and effort at this early stage by handing the salesman a copy of your car-shopping checklist. You will show yourself to be a professional buyer who won't be easily influenced or manipulated. And you will be establishing a firm basis for intelligent comparison shopping among car dealers, for each salesman or dealership will actually be bidding on the same car and options.

After you tell him what kind of car you are considering, the salesman will show you a brochure about a model that you specified or about a similar car that fits your requirements well. With this brochure in hand, he will guide you to a model on the showroom floor or other display area. It may not be the color you want or equipped the way you want, but the salesman will point out such optional features mentioned in the brochure.

When you ask a question, the salesman should answer it. If he doesn't know the answer, the professional salesman will say, "I don't have that answer for you right now, but I will get it for you." Then he will either go to somebody who knows the answer or else open the brochure. With help from the brochure he can provide factual information as well as pictures, and will be able to talk about the standard equipment, weight, engine, rear-axle ratio, and other technical features you may want to know about.

During the entire presentation he will try to be sincere and direct, not fawning or pretentious. Today's young and sophisticated buyers are likely to react negatively to a phony who obviously puts on false enthusiasm and exudes charm. In most dealerships salesmen try to avoid the hard sell which many customers strongly resent.

How the Salesman Closes In on You

Always remember that the salesman is taught to start off by mainly listening, not talking. That way, he can plan his strategy and then move in, leading the customer into a positive decision.

As a professional buyer you must therefore learn to shut up and listen, to plan your own strategy and decide what *you*—not a salesman influencing your choice—want to purchase.

The real professional salesman has a number of tried and true questions that have almost always proven effective in getting customers to make verbal decisions that lead toward closing a deal. These are sometimes called "trial" or "assumed" closes, since their tone and content are based on the premise that the customer is buying.

The psychology of the salesman's questioning is to relax you and set a good mood for you to answer questions *his* way. Some salesmen almost hypnotize you, using your own buzzwords. They constantly ask probing questions or make statements about a car you seem to like—until they find a special one that motivates you and holds your attention. It is then asked or said over and over, with variations, until you are almost in a daze.

Then they move in for the kill, asking questions that you can answer only with a yes: "Isn't this a nice color?". . ."Aren't you impressed with this headroom?". . ."Can you hear the purr of that motor? . . ."

With his mesmerizing succession of adroit questions, the salesman might get your head nodding up and down until you finally nod yes—and sign on the dotted line.

Here are some common examples:

- "Earth tones are very popular and in great demand. Do you like brown or green?"
- "Would you prefer to have your payment fall due on the first, the fifteenth, or the thirtieth?"
- "Do you want to pick it up this afternoon or this evening?"
- "If we can get it in red, will you buy right now?"

Remember, in order to end up with the deal and the car you want, you need to be just as much on your toes as the salesman is. Never forget for a moment that the salesman aims to seize total control of the selling situation. He will attempt to consolidate his position with statements like "Let's go!" or "Come with me."

The salesman likes to give commands and march off purposefully without looking back, leaving you no alternative—he thinks—but to meekly follow him. Therefore, you must be prepared to turn the situation around so that *you* are the one in control.

The main thing is to stay on the salesman's heels . . . not just when he wants you there, but also when he doesn't. For example, when the salesman takes your deal to the manager, follow him! If you are asked to wait, just say firmly and assertively that you would like to speak with the manager yourself. At most dealerships, this will really confuse the entire sales staff because they will be unable to say no.

Arizona's Sophie Surefoot says, "Fine, call me when you talk to your manager," and she heads for her car. This always stops the salesman in his tracks, begging Sophie not to leave.

Ways to Get You to Buy against Your Best Interests

Be alert to a few perfectly legal techniques often used by salesmen to close a deal.

Nowadays, a customer's car keys are no longer hurled onto the roof of a dealership or "accidentally" misplaced by an overeager and unethical salesman. They use subtler and more effective tactics.

TAKING THE CAR HOME

The technique of letting a car sell itself is still popular and widely practiced. If you live in a nice, stable neighborhood near the dealership, the salesman often urges you, pleads with you, all but forces you to take the car home and show it to your spouse, friends, neighbors, and relatives while you're thinking it over.

Once you get the car home, the fun really begins. You take your family on a short ride. Your neighbors flock around to look admiringly and probably enviously at the new car you're getting, your kids are thrilled, your relatives are proud of you, and your spouse acts as if this is the first intelligent thing you've done all year—or maybe during your entire marriage.

In this atmosphere, it can be pretty hard to admit that you haven't actually *bought* the car. So you smile, enjoy the compliments, and—if you're like 85 percent of the "take-homers"—you soon become an owner. For a certain price, of course, which is unlikely to be the one you planned to pay.

Be cautious about that pleasant offer to take any car home. That brief joy ride can cost you dearly. For you have lost your bargaining power.

IGNORING YOUR QUESTIONS

Some dealers actually train their salesmen to ignore a customer's questions. For example, a prospect says, "The dealer down the street has a lower price than yours." The salesman says nothing, or "That's what we hear," and changes the subject. The prospect comes back with, "How can his price be lower than yours?" The salesman ignores him. Finally, the prospect might say, "I don't understand how he can charge so much less than you do." Forced to the wall, the salesman replies with something noncommittal, such as "We don't either."

Somewhere in this dialogue, a prospect *should* say, "Apparently you didn't hear my question. Will you please answer it?" If there still is no satisfactory answer or an attempt to accommodate your interest in bargaining, you had better hotfoot to the place down the street.

CHALLENGING THE CUSTOMER'S MASCULINITY

Another ploy might be called the "Are you a *man?*" dodge.

This is used only when all else fails. It often works well with a man who says he has to talk to his wife before he buys anything.

The salesman puts the choice in the form of a challenge to the prospect's manliness. He asks sarcastically, "Do you mean you have to get your wife's permission? Come on, you're more of a man than that. You *look* like a man's man." If the customer is really a diehard male chauvinist, he'll say, "Give me that paper. Where do I sign?"

A variation with a timid person might be, "Isn't it time you start making your *own* decisions?"

THE CALL-A-SPOUSE ROUTINE

When he is probing for an opportunity to close the deal and finds a customer who uses his or her spouse's absence as an excuse for not buying now, a sharp salesman may dial the number at which the customer's spouse can be reached.

Here's one scenario:

The spouse answers the telephone and the salesman says, "Mrs. (or Mr.) Customer, your husband (or wife) is here at Four Wheels Dealership and wants your permission to buy a car. He (or she) just wants you to say it's okay."

Then he turns to the customer and says, "Your wife (or husband) says it's up to you." If that does not get a signature, he looks into the customer's eyes and continues talking to the spouse on the phone. "Mrs. (or Mr.) Customer, tell your husband (or wife) that you give your permission. He (or she) wants to hear your own voice. My, you're lucky to have a husband (or wife) devoted to getting your opinion before buying! It's so nice to see people who really *love* each other."

MAKING PERSISTENCE PAY OFF

A really hungry salesman might even follow you home or stop by your home hoping to close the deal. Some cars have been sold in the customer's home at 4 A.M., with the people begging to go to sleep and the salesman insisting that he'll leave just as soon as they sign the papers. "I need to have this deal on the manager's desk at eight-thirty A.M. or no deal," he will say. Exhausted, they'll finally sign.

The day after an unsold customer has managed to slip through his grasp, a salesman may call him a dozen times or more if he is positive that he is "hot." The only way one can get rid of him is to say either, "Look, quit calling. I'll never buy a car from you," or "Please come over and write up the order. You sure are persistent."

No salesman has ever been punched in the nose over the telephone, but many have been shouted at or have had a phone slammed down in their ears. This response has discouraged some weak clerks (salesmen who are not true professionals), but it has also often cost the manufacturer, the dealer, the manager, and the salesman himself a sale.

If you are fortunate enough to have a persistent yet unobnoxious salesman, be prepared for all his tactics. Remember when you enter a dealership's showroom that you have come into the salesman's territory. He is used to being in control there. But go in with your own questions, knowledge, plan, a pleasant yet firm smile, and deliberately *enigmatic* silence. . .and *you* can be the one who seizes control and then keeps it.

So enjoy the show a pro salesman puts on—but stick to your plan!

Getting Ready to Make a Deal

Make certain that the salesman knows exactly what you are shopping for. Give him a copy of your filled-out checklist, based on the one provided in Chapter 4.

Wherever you go, be sure that you give out the same checklist—even though you may want to alter some of the specifics later. After all, you'll want all of the salesmen you contact to be bidding on the same items. If some salesmen have been given prices on one set of options and others on another, you would have mass confusion on your hands later on.

After you have given him a chance to look over your list and show you what he's got to fill your needs, the salesman will give you a price. Ask firmly in a friendly manner, *"Is that your best price?"*

Take a notebook with you and write down everything that seems important in the transaction, particularly prices. The salesman will see that you are a no-nonsense buyer.

Be sure that the car you want will be available when you return to a dealership to buy. If your dealer has already sold the particular model you want, he should be willing to obtain another quickly from an associate. (Dealers trade cars with one another, Chevy for Chevy, Ford for Ford, and so on.)

Taking the Test Drive

Don't be shortchanged during your visit to a dealership. Show the salesman that you expect the full treatment even though you may not be prepared to sign a contract to buy.

If you are seriously looking at cars, you will want to drive any that interest you. In fact *never* buy a car without having had a good session or two behind the wheel. If you can't test the actual car you will buy, at least try another one very much like it.

Insist on a demonstration ride. And put your own hands on the steering wheel. Take time to get to know the car; don't be afraid to ask a lot of questions. Although all salesmen are trained to ride with you on a demonstration drive, many dealers will actually let you take a "demo" out on your own. They may even urge you to take it home overnight so everybody you know can get excited about it too. (But, remember, I warned you not to take them up on this.)

This test driving should come only after you are convinced of your ability to handle the sales situation with real aplomb. After considering what to look for in a car and making essential decisions about features and options, you'll be more prepared to go out on a test drive. Then you'll discover whether you are well satisfied. As you know, often things that look good on paper turn out to be otherwise in reality.

So before you take your test drives, prepare your own checklist, based on the pointers here, to remind you of all you need to know while you're inspecting the car and trying it out. Don't be swayed from your basic concerns.

On Your Test Drive

Make careful notes on each car that you look at closely and take out on a test drive. You will be scrutinizing its safety features, its comforts and conveniences, its appearance inside and out.

Before, during, and after the test drive (demonstration), you will ask about:

- Its price to you (and get this down in writing, after the salesman reads your shopping list).
- Its probable maintenance and insurance costs.
- Delivery time.
- Fuel economy—and although you'll be told about it, you should investigate the miles-per-gallon figures on your own to be sure of their reasonable accuracy. All new cars have estimated city, highway, and combination fuel consumption figures on the window price list.

Overall Issues

- Make sure you really like the quality and design of the car. (Remember, you'll be living with it for a long time!)
- Make certain that you test drive a car model similar to the one you are considering—especially one that has the same drive train (engine and transmission combination).
- Drive under the same conditions in which you ordinarily drive. See if the car has enough power to pass slower vehicles and keep up with others. If you usually drive in a hilly area, make sure you do the same on the test.
- Whether you are driving by yourself or with your salesman, keep in mind how many people will normally be riding in your car. If it is to be for family use, make sure there is enough room for everybody to travel in reasonable comfort.
- At the same time, ponder what adding luggage would do. Each person and piece of baggage adds weight to the car, takes away from fuel economy, and makes the car go slower.
- Remember that if the car already borders on being sluggish on

your test drive, any added weight might make you a very unhappy owner indeed, ready to trade for more power. Such quick trading could be very costly.

General Safety and Convenience

Here are things to look for:
- Are the controls on the dashboard easy to locate, identify, and operate during both day and night? Are there any sharp protruding knobs and decorations? Is it padded where a person's face, knees, or chest might hit in an accident?
- Is the steering wheel properly padded? Retractable?
- Are the headrests adjustable so they can be set properly for different people? (These are not so much for comfort but safety, to protect against whiplash.)
- Are there any sharp edges on the doors? Are the doors and pillars padded?
- Are there enough seatbelts and are they properly located? Are they easy to use and comfortable? Do the seatbelts in the front seat also have the holding straps for the upper torso?
- Where is the fuel tank? Is it situated so that a back-end collision will not make it leak?
- Are there blind spots when you use the rear-view mirror or when you turn your head in either direction?
- Can you get a right side-view mirror?
- Can you get a rear-window defogger?
- When the turn signals are turned on, do the side markers flash?
- Can you easily get at the spare tire and the tire-changing tools?
- Does the car have adequate flashing emergency signals?

After you test drive each car, review your experience. Were you comfortable getting in and out of the car? Were you quite comfortable when *in* it?

How were the starting, acceleration, braking, cornering, turning, steering, backing up? And what about the smoothness of the ride, the noise level, visibility (both through the windows and indirectly through the mirrors)? What does the horn sound like?

Refer to Chapter 4 to make sure that you are checking out all the different items on your shopping list so that you will know exactly what comes, or does not come, with the car you have been test driving.

Let's review one last time the four steps in the car-buying process:

1. Learn everything you can about the car, such as equipment, options, color choices. Drive it—*really* drive it—with the number of passengers you'll normally carry. If you're buying a 2.0 liter engine, don't test drive a larger capacity engine, such as a 2.8 liter, because you'll probably be disappointed once you take delivery of the smaller one.

2. How much is that car worth to you? How much do you have as a down payment? How much can you afford as a monthly payment? Also, what does the car actually cost the dealer? Start off on the right foot with your salesman. Be nice but be in control. And don't let anybody talk down to or intimidate you.

3. Try out the service department. Is some customer there screaming, "I've had this car in here twenty times! If you don't fix it this time, I'm going to drive it right through that wall!"? Look around the service department. If it's clean and inviting and they have proper diagnostic equipment, they'll probably give you good service. If they are light on equipment—in the industry this is called "tennis shoes"—they'll "tennis-shoe" you right out of the service department if you really need help. Also, meet the dealer. Just introduce yourself and say, "I've decided I'd like to buy a car here because of your reputation." If he won't come out to talk with you, chances are nine out of ten he won't come out when you need help, either. You may not need serious service after the sale—but you just *might*.

4. Use your God-given, inalienable right of freedom of speech. Negotiate! Interest rates are negotiable, as are many insurance rates. Don't accept what somebody tells you. Keep asking until you're sure you have received the lowest rate possible on both insurance and finance. Always ask what the APR (annual percentage rate) is.

Here's a for instance: A man from Louisville, Kentucky, was told by the salesman that his interest rate was 13 percent. When he received his papers a few days later, he saw that the APR was 22.35 percent. He asked the salesman what that meant and was told,

"Don't worry about that, it's just APR." But he did worry, so he went in to see the sales manager. Well, they rewrote the finance contract, and his car payments were reduced $30 to $40 a month for 42 months!

It's this type of salesman who gives the auto industry a black eye. This tactic is no different, really, from going into a bank with a gun and holding up a teller, except that here the people are trusting. This customer saved over $1,200 just by asking and not accepting what he was told by someone he should have been able to trust.

NOTES:

NINE

Closing the Deal

Baltimore's Willing Millie, a rookie saleswoman, showed Hedy and Slim Mulkey the line of new cars. Having decided on their dream car, a Volcano Flash, the couple settled into Millie's office.

Millie asked for $5,300 and their Spit-Fire. The Mulkeys counteroffered $4,000 and their trade-in.

On the sales order Millie wrote: "Customer offers $4,000 difference." Slim signed it and gave Millie a $100 deposit to show their sincerity.

Millie went directly to the sales manager. "Millie," Gary said, "we've got an acceptable deal. However, I'm going to help you sharpen your rapier for the mental dueling in salesmanship. I'll teach you how to cement the deal yet get more gross profit at the same time."

So Gary wrote across the deal, in green ink: "Mr. and Mrs. Mulkey, you are wonderful people and we appreciate your offer. But we need $4,989.19 difference."

Slim read the note and said to Millie: "I'll give you forty-two hundred." Millie changed the figures. And the "sting" was on.

Gary wrote back: "Happy Valentine's Day—$4,969.09." Again Slim raised his offer—to $4,400 now. Gary's message: "Help me, Hedy. We need $4,961.39."

Hedy finally said to Slim: "We will make it forty-six hundred and that's our final offer."

Up to this point, Gary as desk manager stayed in his own office. Now he came out and met the Mulkeys face to face. After further negotiations, Gary threw in a $300 rustproofing (which actually cost the new car department $70). The agreed-upon difference was now $4,889.19.

The Mulkeys, persuaded now that they had gotten a good buy through shrewd bargaining, left happily—never suspecting that they could have purchased their Volcano Flash for their original offer of $4,000 or even less.

Buying a car can be fun if you learn to enjoy the psychological warfare between buyer and seller.

You've prepared yourself well for your actual entry into the automobile showroom. You've investigated prices, you are sure you can obtain financing, and by now you have already made trips to check on the possible deals available in dealerships. Perhaps you have even made what seems to be a satisfactory contact with a salesman—or several of them, if it looks as if you can get dealerships to compete with each other for your business.

As yet, though, you are wholly uncommitted to any car, from anyone. You are still open to negotiations in order to get the best possible deal for yourself.

Are you a total novice who has carefully studied and rehearsed the preparatory program for bargaining outlined in the last chapter? Or do you already have sufficient experience and self-confidence to allow you to dicker over a deal without having to follow a precise script?

Whatever you are, by now you're finally ready to buy that car you've been aiming to get.

How Deals Are Made

After you have compared prices offered by various dealerships and have talked with your bank or credit union about how these prices stack up with realistic values and dealer costs, it's time to sift through the bids. You can straighten out any questions by telephone, and then—best deal in hand—set out again.

By this time you have probably concluded that there is no such

Thru these portals pass the world's greatest salespeople.

thing as The Best Deal. And you probably are right. If you went to ten dealers and asked for the best price on the same car with identical equipment, you might get different answers on different days—sometimes even from the same dealership. It mostly has to do with the peculiarities of timing. So do this research in as short a time as possible.

Examine all the figures you have gathered to find what seems to be the best deal—which takes into account not simply price and some add-ons, but also your impressions of the quality of service and personnel. Then you'll want to return to do the final bargaining.

Want to Buy the Demonstrator?

Many salesmen will try to get you to buy the demonstrator car itself. Should you buy it if offered to you? Well, if you really do *like* it—and if they offer you a good deal in buying it. (Don't buy it without negotiating. And remember, don't act like an eager beaver. Try to hide or smother your genuine enthusiasm, or you're a dead duck, ready to be laid away by some salesman.)

Remember, a demo could, or should, have all the luxury features. This is where the emotions take over—but don't let them. Be sure that this is *really* what you wanted, and that you can afford to buy it according to your prearranged plan.

A true company demo should be almost perfect, with no squeaks or rattles, good body alignment, and no bugs to work out, since it has already seen action and had essential adjustments. It should be as clean as the table you eat from and a dream to drive. There should be no sign that other people have driven it, such as junk in the trunk.

Note the mileage on the demo. And find out how much of the initial warranty remains on it, in terms of mileage or time. This could be an important factor in making a deal.

If you do decide to buy a demonstrator, ask for an extension of the dealership's guarantee if any remains. And before you take delivery, ask for the warranty extension application and make sure it is filled out accurately. See it with your own eyes and be sure that it gets mailed. Do not trust that it will be taken care of, since the dealership could misplace it or forget to send it in.

Double Dealing

Double dealing gives the auto industry—or any other business—a bad reputation with consumers. Here's a story I call "Silk Purse—or Sow's Ear?"

A legal secretary bought a beautiful, popular-model, near-new car as a dealership demonstrator. After driving it for a short period, a scratch revealed another color under the paint. Her diligent investigation of the car's history brought out the truth—revealing *a total lie*. She found out that it had been purchased by the dealership from a Milwaukee man who had put two wrecked cars—a 1980 and a 1981—together to make one car. This man later told me the story himself. (When I asked which year serial number he used, his answer was, "My mother didn't raise any fools. The '81, of course!") He had gone in, he said, to purchase a brand-new car from a Milwaukee dealer. While starting to explain to the salesman that the car had been repaired extensively although it looked perfect, the salesman stopped him. "I'll give you $5,000 for it," the salesman said. Since he had less than $3,000 invested in the pieced-together car, the man didn't argue but used it as high-value trade-in credit. Then this very reputable, highly profitable, and successful Milwaukee new-car dealership resold this car, as if it were brand new, to someone they thought was gullible. She wasn't. The dealership quietly purchased the car back from her, so the incident never became public. *Caveat emptor:* Buyer beware!

Consider What Others Don't Seem to Want

While you shouldn't compromise your plan more than you really want to—or need to—you owe it to yourself to look at the cars that are not moving so well. You may be able to get a better deal on a particular model simply because the public is not buying it in quantity. Popular models in high demand will sell for list price or even over it at times. Better deals can be made on cars that are overstocked, the don't-wanters.

A don't-wanter is a vehicle the dealer or sales manager is eager to move for a variety of reasons: in stock too long, too many in inventory, wrong equipment, too much equipment, not enough equipment, high-priced, factory incentive programs (manufacturer rebates to dealers for selling slow-moving cars), unpopular color or color combination (which may actually suit you).

If it's a demo, it may have too many miles on it. How many miles are too many has to be decided by you. Smart dealers generally have a policy: to sell a demo before 5,000 miles or ninety days . . . whichever comes first. Unfortunately, some are driven for 10,000 to 30,000 miles.

Another reason a dealer might be eager to sell a particular car could be the high cost of money. Probably 99 percent of the dealers have to borrow in order to finance the cars they have in stock.

On 1982 models, the General Motors Acceptance Corporation offered G.M. dealers the option of $7\frac{1}{2}$ to 10 percent interest floor-plan costs (instead of approximately 17 percent prime rate plus 1 percent). Usually after six to twelve months any unsold cars would go back on prime rate plus 1 percent. Such additional costs could well persuade a dealer to cut prices for a customer willing to take a don't-wanter.

The dealership's need to move the car may play right into your hands. Don't, however, depart too far from your plan. A don't-wanter can be a bargain only if it's what you *really* want after considering all other possibilities.

Cashing In on Dealer Needs

Sometimes a dealer is willing to make a "short deal" (sell at a low price) to help a salesman meet a quota or just to get some action. Or you may find a dealer who is openly hungry for cash or your future service business.

A few quick sales may be needed for cash flow by a dealer for various reasons: heavy or consistent losses on sales versus overhead, too many dollars tied up in used cars or parts and accessories, bad outside investments, a high number of outstanding accounts receivable, poor management, or even embezzlement.

There is some risk in doing business with such dealers, even though their deals may look appealing. They may be in bankruptcy or out of business by the time you need service or make a claim on your warranty service. Your new car warranty, of course, is good at any franchise dealer of a like make. Your used car warranty, however, is good only at the dealership at which you bought the car—unless you purchase a warranty through a reputable insurance company.

Sometimes dealers know they are insolvent but are too embarrassed or afraid to admit it—even to themselves, much less to a customer. At any rate, be careful in taking advantage of a dealer's position so that you are not, in the end, taken advantage of yourself.

In order to calculate the sort of offer you should make—which is lower than what you'd be willing to pay after a round of negotiating, but not so low as to be ridiculous or insulting—refer to Chapter 5's guidelines about car prices to dealers. Figure that your offer should allow for some necessary profit on their part, but make it well below the sticker price.

Go back to the showroom where you got the best price and say to the salesman, *"I can't say your car isn't worth that kind of money. It's just that I can't afford to spend that much."* Don't downgrade the product or disparage the system. Just be straightforward and say, "I'll give you $XXX."

Make that sentence sound as if you are giving a pint of blood. And be sure to use the word "give." When you say "I'll pay," that's money and business talk. But when you say "I'll give," it becomes like flesh and blood—something taken from you which is going to hurt!

You might also want to emphasize your intention to buy at once by using one of those Seven Sets of Seven Magic Words suggested in Chapter 8: "I want to buy a car today."

Tell the salesman to discuss your offer with his sales manager or dealer. If a counteroffer is proposed, study it and answer, "I still can't go that high." Continue to sit on your offer or else suggest splitting the difference between their offer and yours.

Always radiate an air of confidence. But also appear interested in those with whom you are dealing. You might say something like, "I don't expect you to lose money. This has to be a good deal for all of us."

Buyers' Trial Closes

Study the salesman's manner, and when you think the time is right, wrap up the conversation with, "Shall I come back at a more convenient time, or can I take delivery today?" Or try, "I would like my payments to fall due on the fifteenth." (Or the 1st or the 30th or any other day convenient to you.) Or, "Do you want a check or cash on the down payment?" That turns the tables and puts the initiative on your side, to back up your low offer.

If you have impressed the salesman with your preparation and forcefulness, he may now start writing up the deal. (Remember that magic phrase, "Let's see how that looks on paper.")

Don't miss any opportunity while they are writing this up to get a last concession. Try a comment like, "Pardon me, but I assume that this deal includes the AM/FM stereo". . .or the cruise control or some other desirable option.

Remember that the salesman may be as tired as you and just as anxious to close the deal. He might well think that he represented the sale to you with the addition you have just mentioned, so at the last minute he may throw it (or them) in too.

Or you might venture this approach: "Okay, I know you are giving me this car for factory invoice plus fifty dollars, but there are a few more things I need with it, at cost, please." And now is the time for any tricky last-minute trade-in negotiating, if you've put it off until now. Such as, "Oh, I've just decided to trade in my Flame over there. So come on—I'll give it to you for a thousand dollars trade-in from this price."

You never know how much you can accomplish until you *try*.

Closing Techniques

In an automobile sale, there is not just one close (final negotiation, down to the signing of the deal) but often a number of them, generally three.

The first close is the most crucial, since it is the one that seals the deal. There are three different ways for a dealership to approach it. They depend on the person opposite you who handles the last part of the bargaining. These can be the salesman, who may do all of the negotiating with you; the closer, a person who takes over the negotiations after the salesman has mostly sold you on a car; or the desk manager, who might correspond with you about the purchase if you've gone home without buying.

All of the price quotes are recorded on a worksheet. The first person who asks the questions is the salesman. If a deal is not made

by him, a closer (many times referred to as a manager) sits down
and works with the figures and repeats the process. If he can't do it
to everyone's satisfaction, the desk man gets involved. In the end,
in any case, everything is brought to the desk manager, who writes
the order.

Then the payments will be worked out. Monthly payments are
first quoted for short-term financing, then midterm financing, and
finally long-term financing.

WHEN THE SALESMAN ALONE CLOSES

When only the salesman negotiates with you, the session can go
on for hours if you allow it to. Test your offer by saying, "This is all I
have budgeted and I simply cannot pay anymore. This is the only car
I want. If I can't have this one, I'll continue to drive my old car."
Or—what is sometimes dramatically effective—"Well, I'll just have
to shop around."

If the salesman will not negotiate to your liking, thank him, get up,
and walk out. Or ask to talk to the manager or dealer. If none of
them will negotiate on your offer you may have to leave, asking
them to call you if they change their mind. Be sure you talk to the
dealer directly if this is your decision. Tell him that you had selected
his dealership but now are not satisfied with the price or conditions.

THE CLOSER

Closers are sometimes used by dealerships that cannot attract or
keep high-quality salesmen. The purest form of the system prevails
in southern California. It is the quickest, highest gross profit closing
system in the automotive world.

In a typical California-style high-pressure close, the closer will
make you only three offers, in each category. The dialogue goes
something like this:

When the customer asks what the price of the car is, the closer
replies: "Eighty-nine eighty-three and nineteen cents. Write me a
check."

If the customer says, "No, I want a better deal," the closer says,
"I don't know whether I can or not, but if I give you a one percent
discount, I know we can do business, can't we?"

And if that doesn't work, he makes a second offer: "I don't know if

I can or not, but if I give you *another* one percent discount, I know we can do business, can't we?"

Then, if the response is still negative, the closer sighs deeply and says, "All right. Now I'm really going to pull out all the stops. I don't know if I can or not, but if I can get you an additional five percent discount, I know we can do business, can't we?"

At this point you may or may not make an offer depending on how close you are to the deal you had in mind.

If the customer agrees to any of the above deals, the closer moves on to the down payment. First he will ask for 50 percent down. If the response is negative, he'll ask for one-third down. If negative again, he'll ask for 25 percent down.

The next step is the trade-in. The amount offered is $1,000 to $2,000 under the wholesale value of the car. If the customer balks at these offers, the closer will offer $100 more. If the customer doesn't want to accept the offer, the closer will offer another $100 two more times.

The technique of the California-style close is unnervingly powerful. A salesman can be readily trained to overpower a customer. The rapid machine-gun questions are calculated to be shocking—to get a person rattled and off track and induce him or her to buy quickly without giving any thought to real price or value.

So beware!

THE DESK MANAGER

Before you sign a sales order, approach and talk directly to the desk manager, who is the one who writes up the final purchase order papers at some dealerships. You might not ever meet him otherwise—even though he's the one with whom you would probably be carrying on various negotiations through notes carried back and forth by the salesman.

If you visit a dealership but cannot work out a purchasing arrangement, often the desk manager will take over from the salesman in pursuing you. Short notes may be passed to you time after time until an agreeable deal is arrived at—or you have been worked over for the final dollar.

You may say, "This is my offer, period," or "This is my *final* offer." However, the desk manager will still keep trying, often using the salesman as a buffer. His notes may read like this:

- (Your name): We sincerely appreciate your offer and sincerely want your business. However, we need $XXX.
- Happy Birthday! (or Valentine's Day, Easter, Fourth of July, Thanksgiving, Holidays).
- Good Today Only! This is a dynamite deal!
- Offer good until we make five deals like this one.
- Let's split the difference.
- We really want to sell a car in your neighborhood (or company or city).
- We've already sold to your neighbors (or fellow employees or club members).
- You are a very influential person and know a lot of people. We want you as a customer and therefore wish to make a deal with you.
- We really need your business because your deal will help us win a manufacturer's contest.
- We'll give you that other car at the old price. We'll take off the wire wheels, put in this radio instead of that one, throw in rustproofing, body-side moldings, paint stripes, vinyl roof. . .TV, vacation, dinner, theater or ballgame tickets.

The Second Close

When you shop around, you obtain prices based on the standard model being marketed. The professional salesman, in most negotiations, does not discuss the items listed below until you have agreed on the price of a car, signed the order, and given a deposit.

Please remember to use your shopping list and make sure that everything is on your order before you sign and commit yourself. Also remember to include your weasel clause.

At this point you must tell the salesman, "This is all the equipment I want. Period." If you don't he will start selling all over again. So make sure that you are getting everything you wanted in making your deal.

If certain equipment or accessories important to you aren't expressly included in your car deal, the selling begins again. This new negotiating is called "after market." It includes these dealership-installed or -prepared features:

- Rustproofing

- Undercoating
- Special audio equipment
- Interior car protection (carpeting and upholstery)
- Exterior car protection (paint and chrome protection)
- Floor mats
- Special tires
- Special wheels
- Special flat-tire protection
- Body-side moldings
- Vinyl roof
- Paint stripes
- Cruise control
- Air conditioning
- Litter containers

If your plan is complete, all of the extras should be in the deal you have negotiated. But if you have forgotten something or want to add something at this late date, use common sense. After you have virtually *bought* the car, these items can be quite costly. Generally no uniform list price exists among dealerships on the after-market items, and the markup price can be very high—up to a 300 percent profit margin. Some dealerships offer special package prices which still contain a tremendous built-in profit.

Many customers buy after-market items from an auto supply store, tire store, so-called discount store, or auto salvage yard, and install them themselves, usually at appreciable savings. You'll know what is best for you.

The Third Close

With the second close over, you can relax. Briefly.

Expect the selling to start again as soon as you are turned over to the finance and insurance division or to the business manager. The words "finance" and "insurance" are usually camouflaged, to help you stay relaxed but ready to spend more.

Here is what will be discussed with you, particularly if the dealership is in the financing and insurance sales business. They'll try to sell you as much as you're willing and able to go for. And though you may resent the prospect of shelling out more money, these matters should be considered:

- Financing arrangements
- Mechanical breakdown insurance
- Credit life insurance
- Accident and health insurance
- Collision insurance
- Public liability and property-damage insurance (if state law permits dealers to handle)

Reneging on the Deal

Check again that you have cash available for your down payment and future installment payments worked out.

It's so easy to get off the track while wheeling and dealing over a car that it is wise to recheck your facts and figures often. How does the final deal compare with what you had intended to get?

Before you sign on the dotted line, don't be embarrassed to back off if you decide that this deal is not right for you. The dealer will recover. If necessary, you can use a handy excuse to delay committing yourself, such as: "I'm not ready to sign yet," "I have to check this out with my wife," or "I always sleep on a big decision."

If you do sign, add a weasel clause like: "This deal is subject to financing terms acceptable to buyer." It will allow you time to sleep on the deal or talk it over with someone.

How to Say No

Beware if the salesman tries the Plus and Minus system. Your salesman might draw a line down the middle of a paper and put + on one side and − on the other. On the left side you'll set down the reasons why you should buy a car, and of course your selling companion really helps you fill it out. He'll let you do the minus side all by yourself, because these are your objections as to why you shouldn't buy that car right now.

If you won't sign on the dotted line, a salesman is trained to find out what your objections are. And you've helped him out by conveniently providing him with your list of reasons as to why you're not buying. Now he'll counter them by giving you at least one positive reason why you should buy for every negative reason. And you may well end up ignoring your hesitancy, which was there for your own good.

Don't ever allow yourself to feel trapped by this clever and persuasive strategy. If you don't want to buy the car and are anxious to escape the clutches of his hard or soft sell, just say, *"I don't know why, but I just don't want to buy."* Don't say anything else. Repeat it as many times as you have to.

Never be reluctant, afraid, or embarrassed to say *no, no, no!* to anyone involved in the car-selling process. You may even have to walk out of the showroom, taking your principles *and* your hard-earned dough!

Get It in Writing!

After you agree to a total and final price for everything, be sure that the manager, dealer, or the proper dealership-appointed person signs, dates, and accepts the deal. Also make certain that:

- You have a receipt for your money.
- You have an exact copy of the buyer's order with all the figures filled in as you agreed. Also, that the order is signed, dated, and accepted by the manager, dealer, or their official representative.
- All the equipment is listed: the model number, color, stock number, and serial number.

As a precaution, write down the serial number of the car (you can find it on the driver's side of the dashboard at the base of the windshield). Then match it to the one that is written on your order. This ensures that you will receive the car you ordered if you're buying one already in stock that you examined and test drove.

Be aware that car switching is a bad business practice among unscrupulous salesmen or dealers. They will also remove things you ordered and replace them with unwanted items or things of lesser value. If you inadvertently approve such a switch, it becomes legitimate.

So write down the brand name and size of the tires (including the spare tire), type of wheels if special (mags, wire, spokes), audio brand name and type (stereo, AM/FM, CB, 8-track, cassette), battery, and alternator. Be sure they are listed on the order by these brand names and serial number or other descriptions.

I only mention these rare, unsavory practices. But please don't harbor suspicions against *all* retail auto pros. Fortunately, unethical pros represent a small percentage of the car sales business.

If you give your consent to a delivery date later than the one originally agreed upon, be sure to get all of the particulars in writing.

Getting Your Car at Last

All the final papers and money involved in car buying are usually signed and exchanged at the dealership. However, sometimes you will complete a purchase at your place of business or home.

Almost all cars are picked up at the dealership by the customer. The rare exception is when the salesperson helps you surprise someone with a gift car by driving it for you to your home or some other place of your choice. This way you can arrange for your generous gesture to take a big bow at a birthday, anniversary, or holiday.

Having successfully negotiated your car purchase, you should now be a wiser and far more informed buyer. In all your transactions, continue to be courteous and exercise good judgment and common sense. Don't let your new skills swell your head.

Treat your new car with tender loving care. It will pay off during your long companionship and when you reluctantly trade it in for another car—you will bargain with even greater knowledge and self-confidence when making deals on wheels.

NOTES:

What you see in a salesman might not be what you think you see.

TEN

Buying a Used Car

Some time ago, at Don McCullagh Chevrolet in Detroit, Boot-Nose Cunningham approached the new customer who was walking through the used car lot. "How can I help you, son?" was the way he greeted him.

In response, Handsome Harry handed the salesman a note informing him that he was a deaf mute.

Unable to speak persuasively to this customer or get *him* to talk (a salesman's prime objective with a customer), how in the world was Boot-Nose going to make a sale?

Frustrated, Boot-Nose scurried away and told the manager about his unusual predicament. "Just stick with him," the manager advised, "and see what he wants to buy. You can *write*, can't you?"

Hog-Jaws Siegfried, overhearing the conversation, got a big laugh out of his old rival's situation. "Just watch me make a sale," Boot-Nose snarled at him.

Boot-Nose trailed Harry as he walked slowly around the lot, carefully inspecting all the merchandise. Finally Harry pointed to a four-door Sea-Rider. Then he produced a pencil and notepad and wrote a short message: "How much for this car?"

Looking around, Boot-Nose saw Hog Jaws looking at him in

amusement. He'd show *him* and the manager too that he could write as well as talk. So he wrote, "$3,899."

His customer wrote back, "I will give you $3,000."

After a few more notes and a test drive, they compromised— much in Harry's favor—at $3,100. Hog-Jaws was not impressed. But Boot-Nose at least had managed to make his sale.

Harry was not only firm in holding his bargaining position, but his unfortunate disability actually worked to his benefit.

The same moral pertains to used car buying as to new: Car buyers would do well to neither speak nor listen! Reduce communications to a bare minimum when dealing with a salesman.

Some people have never bought a new car. They are much more concerned about economizing than about possessing a car in the latest style and in pristine condition. Having always found a used car that satisfied their needs, they do not feel that the far greater expenditure for a new car is merited.

Many people, though, have no other choice. The only set of wheels they can afford has already been owned and driven. This seems to be increasingly true for a large number of car buyers.

If you have decided to buy a used car, watch out! It can look like the most intelligent thing to do—and it well might be for you. *Yet if you don't do your homework, you may end up paying the same price for a used car as you would for a new car.* A lot of people make this expensive mistake.

Many people who are faced with the prospect of buying a used car, perhaps for the first time, get panic-stricken at the very thought of buying what may have been the source of another person's woes. Don't be overly fearful of such an unhappy predicament. With good preparation and planning, along with a careful inspection of any car you are seriously considering, you should have an excellent chance of purchasing a car that will serve you well for at least a few years— and, with luck, won't require perpetual, frustrating, and expensive repair work.

Where Are Good Used Cars to Be Found?

When planning on buying a used car, use the same decision-making procedures detailed in earlier chapters for buying a new car. Your primary concerns should be:

• How much can you comfortably spend on the car?

• How much can you put into the down payment?

• How much can you afford to pay in monthly installments?

You should also realize that the interest rate on an older car will probably be higher than on a new car, and the older the car, the higher the rate.

Buying a used car is not at all like buying a new car. Each used car is one of a kind. You can't shop for used cars as easily as you can for new cars, since comparisons are so difficult because of age, body style, color, options, and both odometer miles and mileage (in terms of wear and tear).

Fast-selling used cars are clean as a wolf's tooth—mint!—and in the $2,500 to $4,500 price range—a price that varies according to area, economic conditions, inflation, and availability. It is best to try to buy a used car in a glutted market.

Disasters like tornadoes, hurricanes, and flooding rivers can destroy thousands of cars in the affected communities. Ruined cars must be quickly replaced, causing the price of used cars to sky-rocket as they become scarce. For thirty to forty-five days after a flood, prices can be as much as $2,000 above normal value.

Like a new car, a used car is a major purchase. It requires comparison shopping for price and value. Used cars can be found at new car dealerships, used car lots, and daily rental and leasing companies. Over 50 percent of used car sales are made by private individuals.

Do the natural thing and look where you feel the pickings will be most promising. But you also might find a super buy where you wouldn't really think to go. Check domestic dealers, for instance, for used imports; you could find some surprises there. And check some luxury dealers for nonluxury-class cars; even more pleasant sur-prises might await you there.

I state this in order to point out places where you could find a hidden gem or a "cream puff" at a tremendous buy. Remember, most other used car buyers might never think of going there either. Hence the demand—and the price—may be low.

Probably your safest bet is buying from a friend, who will be honest, fair, and let you know exactly what you're getting. But watch the price! Some friendly favors can cost you dearly. There is always the awkwardness that ensues if the car starts to fall apart after you buy it.

Advantages of Buying from New Car Dealerships

New car dealerships might charge more for a used car, but they usually keep only the best cars that come in as trade-ins. They also have service shops that can do both major and minor servicing before putting a car out on the lot. They will honor any warranty given with a used car, just as they do with new cars they sell.

Independent used car dealers may or may not have a service shop. They, as well as many new car dealers, get used cars from trades and by purchasing from new car dealerships, leasing fleets, police departments, and automobile auctions.

Remember, the longer a used car lot has been in business, the better your chances are for being fairly treated. Nowadays, with the greater attention paid to consumers and their rights, operators whose shady tactics stir up customer ire in the community are not apt to last long. Often, such fly-by-night places are mismanaged. They go for quick and easy money and pay little attention to adequate accounting, even less to improving their public relations.

In the hope of obtaining more information about a car, always ask the dealer for the phone number of its previous owner. If you speak to him or her directly, you can ask *what is wrong* with the car. Your chances of getting an honest answer are much greater than if you ask *whether* there is anything wrong with the car—which usually brings the simple answer "No."

In some states a dealership is required to safety-check each car totally before it is put on the lot to be sold. (This will not be done, of course, in most cases when you buy from an acquaintance or through an ad.) In fact, the Federal Trade Commission tried in 1982 to make this a nationwide requirement for all car dealers, but the measure was defeated in Congress. One of the objections given in testimony at the time was that such a requirement would add too much to the price of a car and would be too costly to enforce.

In most states, therefore, the inspection of a used car is still up to the professionalism of the dealer.

Ask whether the car you are interested in has already been safety-checked. If it has, ask to see the paperwork on it.

Because such an inspection usually is not arranged by a private seller, you really have a better chance of getting a safe, well-functioning car if you get it from a dealer.

Judging the Asking Price

How can you tell if the asking price is fair?

Go to your credit union or local bank and ask to see some of the current publications on wholesale and retail car prices, such as those published monthly and on a regional basis by NADA (National Automobile Dealers' Association), the Black Book or state Blue Book. One of these guidebooks will tell you the average loan value and the current wholesale and retail prices of the car you're considering.

When you buy from a private party, the price will usually be somewhere between the wholesale and retail prices. In many instances, people pay above retail price because they somehow assume they are getting an exceptional buy from an individual seller. Therefore they neither question the asking price nor bargain.

When a dealer can't arrive at an agreeable price with new car buyers, he occasionally tells them to sell the old cars themselves, saying that the sellers can probably get more for their old cars than he could. So keep in mind that sometimes a better buy may be at a dealer's, who will often give a limited guarantee or warranty, too.

As I suggested, if it's possible take the car you are considering to an independent diagnostic service or mechanic for a complete check. If your state has a mandatory car-resale inspection program, have the car inspected immediately before purchase or else specify in the bill of sale that the purchase is conditional on the car's passing the state inspection.

You can also put off the final signing by using any of the other weasel clauses discussed in Chapter 9—("I have to get my wife's approval first," "I really want my mechanic to look at it," "I need to see if I can get the right bank loan," etc.). If you do write the deal down on paper, add "Subject to my wife's (or mechanic's) approval" or "financial terms acceptable to buyer," and so on.

What if There's a Defect in the Used Vehicle You Want?

You might see at a dealership a used car or van that you like but notice that it has something wrong with it. Whether the salesman tells you of the problem outright or admits the condition when you point it out to him, you are in a position now to bargain with him. You should be able to get a low price quote, since you both now recognize either aesthetic or mechanical problems that will require repair or replacement.

In this case, you can certainly consider having repairs made as part of the deal. Many times when a car is worth repairing, the used car manager can get it fixed for far less money than you'd pay yourself. He does this by using outside job shops' salvage yards or a used car mechanic at special dealership labor rates.

Some dealers and executive managers insist that all repairs be done in house. Although there *may be* savings to you as well as convenience in this, make sure that it won't actually cost you more than if you purchased the vehicle at a reduced price and then had it fixed elsewhere, by a mechanic or body shop known to you for quality work.

If you do decide to repair the car, ask the mechanic what alternatives you have—new parts, rebuilt parts, or used parts. How much are they? Then you negotiate.

If the price is more than you can afford, or higher than you think it should be (by checking elsewhere on the phone), negotiate again. If this doesn't get the desired results, ask to speak to the service manager. Explain honestly what is on your mind—and negotiate some more. You might arrive at some other alternatives, and even discover that the repair can be covered under your car's warranty or mechanical-breakdown insurance.

If the repair must be paid from your own pocket, make certain you have the funds or the ability to secure this extra money. Investigate and make arrangements through the dealer's sources or your own.

Always get everything in writing, filled out exactly and completely, including the right date. Also, find out if the dealer's work is guaranteed, and if so, over what period of time and/or how many miles it applies.

One more thing: Check to make certain that the odometer reading is the same when the car is returned to you as it was on the repair order—unless, of course, a little test driving had to be done. Some employee with a carefree spirit might have taken up joy riding in your newly purchased car, without the management's knowledge. In which case, of course, you will want to report the transgression.

The National Highway Administration can be reached by calling 1-800-424-9393. They can tell you if a particular car has any factory recalls.

Taking Over Someone Else's Payments

In purchasing a used car, you will sometimes run into the opportunity to take over a previous owner's payments—often at an interest rate lower than that prevailing at the time of purchase—instead of making totally new financial arrangements of your own.

It sounds good, but is it really a good idea? Actually, in such a situation you would become liable to the lender who gave the loan in the first place. However, the person from whom you are assuming that loan also remains liable to the lender. In this way, the transferred loan many times operates much like a co-signed note.

If you are confident of the parties with whom you are dealing, the assumption of the previous owner's payments may be a good deal for you. It is riskier for the other person, though he may be willing to assume that risk in order to sell his car at a better price and more quickly.

The best that can be said here is to be careful of what you are agreeing to and with whom.

Buying from Private People

Private sellers usually are found through ads in the classified sections of newspapers; others may be friends, relatives, neighbors, or sellers you hear about through the grapevine. (The next chapter about selling your old car suggests ways in which a car for sale can be advertised, sometimes at no cost to the owner.)

Private sellers could have cars that are in worse condition than those at dealerships. . .or they could have perfectly good ones at much better prices than you could get from a dealer.

It is important for you to remember that when you buy a car in an "as is" condition from a private seller, you get no warranty. You will have to obtain your own financing or pay full cash outright for the car. You will also have to take care of all the legal paperwork yourself—although this chore is often shared with the previous owner:

You should also make sure that the mileage is correct on the used car that you are considering buying. (See the section on odometers in Chapter 11.)

Two Cases of Bad Private Deals

Roy Denoyer was looking for a used car. He asked his neighbor where he had bought his recently acquired used car, because he liked it. The neighbor said he had bought it from a certain dealership. Roy said he would never buy a used car from a dealer because lot cars cost too much and because he was sure he could get a better deal from a private party. The neighbor explained that if he bought a car from a dealership and something went wrong with it, he could at least go back there and pursue the matter.

But Roy disregarded this advice and bought a used car from a private party. A month later he had to put in a new oil pump and have some work done on the brakes. When the neighbor inquired about how he liked his new car, Roy told him about his troubles. The neighbor reminded Roy of what he had said earlier about going to a dealership instead of buying privately. Roy said he didn't want to hear any remarks from him, and turned and walked away. So much for good and well-intended neighborly advice!

Then there's the young woman who bought a handsome used car from a private party. She asked some friends (who weren't mechanics) to look the car over before she purchased it. After visually inspecting it, they told her it was in good shape. . . . Then she spent $850 for engine repairs shortly after buying the car!

Don't Fall Into a Stolen-Car Scam

The very worst type of deal on which to get "taken" is buying a stolen car by mistake. This can easily happen to an unsuspecting private party, and it can even happen to a dealer. Some of the thieves involved in stolen-car rings are very clever, using false I.D. numbers and other ruses to get unsuspecting *dealers* to buy their goods.

The important thing to remember when dealing inadvertently with stolen merchandise is that, as a private party, *you* could get stuck with any loss if the car's true owner locates it after a search.

Some dealers carry insurance against this, but private parties do not.

When I had my Milwaukee dealership, a salesman brought in a car, inviting us to buy it from a man who we were told was in a hospital bed. It seemed in good condition, and the price was right, so we bought it outright. Later, while preparing the car to show on the lot, an informant called me, warning of a deception. I drove the car to the police station, where we discovered from tracing the identification that it—or I should say *part* of it, the vehicle's I.D. numbers and title—had belonged to the man who was supposed to be in the hospital, but who had died in the hospital following an automobile accident one year earlier. Yet this car itself was undamaged. *His* car was a Chevrolet Blazer; the car sold to us was a GMC Jimmy disguised with Chevrolet identification, trim, and grille. Our young salesman lied to us.

Law enforcement officers know where to look for hidden I.D. numbers (frame of car, etc.). It turned out that the basic car had been stolen on Tuesday from a Minneapolis dealer's lot. The fellows allegedly involved in a car-theft ring had stripped it of its GMC Jimmy identification and put on the Chevrolet Blazer I.D. from the dead man's car. (The two car models have the same body styles.) They made all other necessary changes in disguising its identity— and then, seven days later, offered the altered car to us for a cash sale. Our young salesman gave our check to a dead man and gave us a title. . .signed by a dead man.

Luckily, we had insurance to cover this difficulty, so the mystery was unraveled with no loss to us but the $100 deductible. But we were a little embarrassed, although we had acted in good faith. Even the most vigilant dealers can't catch all the car crooks that come their way.

Earlier in my career, when I had my dealership in Athens, Ohio, I was not so fortunate. I had to absorb a loss of $900 or so. Again, it was a matter of a stolen car being brought into the dealership and offered to us. A young man identifying himself as a student traded in a car that needed some body work. One of the dealership's body shop repairmen wanted to buy it. We made the sale at a reasonable price and he fixed the car up.

The employee was entirely happy until he went to get a license plate and found that the I.D.'s on the title and on the dash were for a

V-8 engine, not matching the car's six-cylinder engine. A state highway patrolman was called in and found other evidence in hidden serial numbers that further proved that the car must have been stolen. The "student," of course, was long gone by this time, and the loss was the dealership's.

So whatever you do, be careful of having anything like either of these incidents (or the dozens more that I could relate) happen to you.

Checking the Car Out Carefully

You yourself can do quite a lot of inspecting of cars you might wish to buy. Just as with buying a new car, it is extremely helpful to prepare a reminder list of things to examine or test in both the exterior and interior of a car, as well as its working condition. Usually the best buy is a two- or three-year-old car. It's usually not yet old enough to need a lot of costly repairs.

Some general advice:

1. Check the car as thoroughly as you can, inside and out. Read up on the basic working parts of a car and their functions so that you can be somewhat knowledgeable when you test drive it. Be sure to look under the hood, under the frame, at the wheels and tires, and so forth.

2. Shop during the day. Darkness and a used car lot's high-intensity lights may hide problems. However, many high-quality dealership lots are well lit and are designed for a gray day and for evening shoppers.

3. If you are buying a car, especially a used car, do not look at it or test drive it in the rain. Nicks and scratches on the finish can be covered up by the rain, and the wetness of the car's body can make it look shiny and waxed. Also, the noise of the rainfall can cover up small pings or even louder sounds in the engine.

Some states have laws that retract or void the sale contract if a car was sold with an excessively damaged frame, unless the sale was by mutual agreement, with the damage considered acceptable by the buyer.

While shopping for a used car, you should keep a good many things in mind. Look over the checklist provided in Chapter 4 to see whether there are important items you might note down. Review the instructions for a test drive given in Chapter 8. Any defects in performance should be taken seriously, though you'll also have to allow for the car's age and condition and not expect perfection.

Use the following questions and suggestions in preparing your checklist to take shopping with you.

CHECKING THE OUTSIDE

- Look for dents or rust around the bottom of the doors and rear fenders. Rust could be minor if it hasn't gone through the metal. If it has gone through or the metal is pitted, repairs could be expensive. Look under the car for rust. Check the muffler, tail pipe, and exhaust pipe. If a rotten egg smell is apparent or the mileage odometer shows 50,000 miles, a replacement catalytic converter might be needed. Any emission-control item is covered under factory warranty for five years or 50,000 miles, whichever comes first, regardless of how many owners the car has had.
- Look for ripples in the sides and subtle paint shade differences, breaks in the frame, or welding spots on the frame. This could mean that the car was involved in a serious accident or has a weakness in its structure.
- Open and close the doors, hood, and trunk. Be sure they fit and are easy to operate.
- Look under the car for oil spots or fluid leaking from the transmission or shock absorbers.
- Check the shock absorbers by pushing down one corner of the car and letting it go. Repeat this procedure. If the car bounces several times, new shocks may be needed.
- Stand back and see if the car is level. If one corner seems lower than the others, it may mean that a spring is broken or weak.
- Check the tires. See if they are worn or brand new or somewhere in between. In the past, belted tires most likely would last for 25,000 miles of normal driving. Radial tires, which are standard on most cars built in the last few years, should last for 50,000 miles. Uneven tire wear may indicate a need for a front-end alignment, new shock absorbers, or brakes, or that the frame has been bent in an accident. Make sure that all the tires

match. Check the inside of the tires because a badly scuffed tire may have been turned around.

- Grab the top of each front tire and shake it hard, in and out. Clunking noises or a lot of free play may mean worn suspension joints or wheel bearings. This would be expensive to repair. Leakage of brake fluid can be seen on the inside of the tire.

LOOKING AT THE INSIDE

- Open the hood. Check the belts and hoses for cracks or wear. Check the battery for cracks. Pull out the oil dipstick. If the oil is dark and dirty, the previous owner has not properly maintained the car. Check the mileage on the odometer with the lubrication stickers on the door or under the hood to see when the oil and lube were last performed. (If the previous owner did his own oil and lube, there will be no stickers.) Check the automatic transmission fluid. It should be clear and not have a burnt smell.
- Get yourself a screwdriver with a long wooden handle. With the engine running, put the metal part up to an air conditioning compressor or alternator on the car. Using it like a doctor's stethoscope by putting the wooden part to your ear, you can hear if there are any bearings in there making odd noises. (A good mechanic can do this for you too.) Question the noises and just ask, "What is that?" People will think you are a pro. Please don't stick the screwdriver in or through any moving parts.
- Open the trunk. Check the spare and its tread and make sure it's inflated. Uneven wear may mean a front tire was put in the trunk to hide a front-end problem. Make sure that the wheel changing equipment is all there and that it works.
- Check the car interior for worn seats, belts, carpeting, and keys; similarly, check the clutch, brake, and gas pedals. Heavy usage will show here.
- Check the windows to see if they open and close easily. If they don't there may be a problem with the frame, in which case have a mechanic look it over. Check for nicks in the glass.
- Check the glass on the lights. Test all of them or ask the owner or salesman to turn them on in turn while you look. Check the flashers, headlights, taillights, backup lights, turn signals, run-

ning lights. Start the engine and check the warning lights, gauges, radio, heater, horn, window wipers, air conditioner (even in winter), and the overhead lights. Make certain that the air conditioning blows very cold air. If it doesn't, it could require very expensive repairs, or it could just need a Freon gas tune-up.

Remember that you need to *know,* not just *guess,* about the condition of all these car functions. If you find minor problems, calculate how much it would cost to fix them and discount this figure from a used car book price in order to determine a fair offer for the car. For major problems, you must do more serious thinking.

THE TEST DRIVE

- Turn on the radio and change the stations by using the push buttons.
- Start the engine and press down on the brakes for about one minute. If the pedal sinks slowly, there may be a leak in the master cylinder of the brakes.
- When the engine is cold, listen for noises that could indicate engine problems.
- Put the car in neutral and step on the gas. Look in your rear-view mirror and note the color of the exhaust. If there is a lot of white or bluish smoke, the engine may need an overhaul. Idle the engine and listen for noises or vibrations. These could indicate a need for a tune-up or new valves.
- Drive on a flat, smooth road. If the car pulls in any direction, a front-end alignment may be needed.
- When you make right or left turns, the steering wheel should not feel either loose or tight.
- As you drive the car, check the temperature gauge to see if it shows a high reading or if the temperature warning light is on. If it is, stop the car. Shut off the engine and open the hood. Don't remove the radiator cap! Listen for hissing or look for steam escaping or coolant leaking out. These are signs of trouble with the cooling system, and they can be expensive.
- Accelerate to 35 mph and listen for a whine from the rear end. Now accelerate to 45 mph. Check for bouncing or vibrations.

Vibrations at 45 mph may mean that the tires need balancing. Vibrations with a whine may mean a problem with the drive shaft or universal joints.

- If you hear a roaring or groaning noise at 38 mph to 43 mph from the rear of the car, check to see if the vehicle has mud and snow tires. It is best to test a car without these tires. Otherwise you can't be sure where the noise is coming from. Generally such sounds are signs of a bad rear end, which can be a very costly repair.

- Drive briskly over a rough road. Do you hear any loud rattles or squeaks? Is there a steering problem? Does the car bounce or bang around over small bumps? If so, the suspension may be worn. Worn-out ball joints and control arms could cause the car to wander all over the road and will be impossible to correct with a front-end alignment.

- To test the brakes, accelerate to 30–40 mph, but make sure there are no cars behind you. Step hard on the brake pedal, but don't lock the wheels. The brake pedal should not feel spongy, sink too far to the floor, weave, grab, or chatter. And watch for signs of the car's pulling to the right or the left—a telltale indication of the need for brake adjustment, or perhaps something more serious.

- To check the transmission, drive the car forward and backward several times. The clutch in a manual transmission should not grab, have excessive play, or make noise. In an automatic transmission the shift from one gear speed to another, up or down, should be smooth; the transmission should not race, lurch, or hesitate between shifts.

- Accelerate the car to get it into high with an automatic or manual transmission. Release and let the car slow down but not enough to shift down. Then accelerate again, carefully so it doesn't shift. The engine should accelerate smoothly without any noises. Noises may indicate a need for a tune-up or overhaul.

- Check the car's power when going uphill. If there is a power loss, the car may need an overhaul or a tune-up.

- Test out the hand brake on a hill to make sure that it holds the car.

AFTER THE DRIVE

- Check the exhaust tail pipe. A black, sooty oil deposit may mean that the engine burns oil. If the deposit is white and powdery, it usually means good fuel combustion.
- Give consideration to the availability of parts, probable fuel economy, and maintenance costs and insurance.
- Check the odometer mileage to be sure the car hasn't been used too much for the price being asked.

Making Your Decision

If you are pleased with the car's performance and are seriously considering buying it, take it to a mechanic or auto diagnostic service. The mechanic should be your trusted mechanic, not the dealership's. And a diagnostic service is a good place to get an objective opinion. It may cost you $25 to $50 for an inspection, even more for a thorough one, but the expenditure is worth it if it saves you from buying a lemon.

Ask the mechanic the approximate cost of repairing any defects. If you want to buy the car, use this estimate in negotiating for a lower price. Also, read the section in Chapter 11 on "Silent Rejection" and use it to your advantage by taking the salesman's position.

The best place to have the car inspected is at a dealership that handles the same make car because they work on that kind of car every day. It is becoming increasingly difficult for backyard mechanics to work on and diagnose the newer cars because of all the sophisticated equipment, including computerized mechanisms and circuits.

A BIG WARNING: When you take a car to a dealership, someone may try to get you off track. A service writer or a mechanic may act as a bird dog—someone who tips off a salesman or leads him to a possible buyer. Informed that a ripe used car buyer is here, the salesman will try to sell you a car from his dealership's own lot. To get an accurate appraisal of the car's mechanical condition, make sure you tell him that you're not interested.

Anyone going out to buy a used car should realize that he or she is going to have to spend, on the average, $500 for repairs and maintenance within a short period of time. The best advice I can give you is to buy a brand-new car or truck—or as new a one as you possibly can. Some people spend enough money throughout the year on repairs to make new car payments. Of course many people don't have any choice other than to buy a used car, because of their economic or credit situation. But if you must buy a used car, have a mechanic check it over for you. The money spent in checking it over will save you a lot of money and heartache later.

NOTES:

ELEVEN

What to Do with Your Old Car

After reading the original manuscript of this book, Howard, a Washington attorney, told his Uncle Phil, a car dealer, "I want to buy a car today."

And Uncle Phil said, "Fine! For my nephew I'll only charge you fifty dollars over invoice."

Howard replied swiftly, "How much trade-in allowance for my car?"

His uncle told him, "Nineteen hundred dollars."

Howard then smiled and said, "Let's see how it looks on paper. . .but I want to have the option of selling my car and giving you nineteen hundred cash instead of trading it in." Uncle Phil agreed.

Howard tried out three of the surefire zinger ads from this chapter—"must sell" and "cream puff" and "any reasonable offer considered"—and added a brief description of the car and his phone number.

Howard managed to sell his car for $2,700.

"Good for you!" Uncle Phil praised him. Howard essentially paid $800 less for his new car—because he had been paid that much *more* for his old car by handling the selling himself.

So here you are, deciding to buy a new car, or at least a newer one than the one you have been driving. Do you really need to have two cars (or more) in your household? And can you *afford* to keep them both (or all)?

Perhaps you have already thought through your situation quite thoroughly and know exactly how you're going to handle the matter of your old car. But if not, this chapter should provide you with important information and suggestions.

Approaching the Trade-in

Always remember that you are not necessarily locked in to using your car as a trade-in with a dealership from whom you intend to buy a new car. This is one reason I have already advised you to leave your present car out of consideration as a trade-in, at least in preliminary negotiations. Just as you are shopping around for the best price deal on a new car, you can shop around for the best offer for your used car.

And of course you don't have to feel stuck with dealers. To receive the highest dollar amount you might have to sell your used car privately through the newspaper or by placing a For Sale notice in a window. If you do, take your time. It could mean several hundred—or thousand—dollars in your pocket.

Silent Rejection

Don't let a dealership or other buyer weaken your position regarding the value of your car.

When a good salesman looks at a client's trade-in, he won't *say* anything derogatory about the car's appearance. He knows a customer's old car is a close companion to him, maybe his best and most dependable friend for a long time.

When I was a young salesman, a customer asked me jovially how much his nine-year-old Buick was worth. In the same jovial manner I replied, "About as much as I earn taking it to the junkyard—a penny a pound, which is about forty dollars." Needless to say, I did not sell that man a new car. He felt insulted. He had purchased his Buick new and it had served him well. He believed it still had some

I don't want to buy a car!!!

good life in it and was not going to have it talked about that way by anybody!

So when a skillful salesman looks over a trade-in, he makes sure that the customer is standing close by, watching his examination. He wants the customer to conclude for himself that the resulting offer may not add up to much. Deftly, the salesman will run his fingers over the scratches, note the faded paint, and look at the rip in the upholstery. He will linger over any imperfection. This is to let the customer know that *he knows* they're there, and banish any thought the customer might have had of getting top dollar.

If you are sure that your car is in good shape, in spite of a few minor and superficial flaws, don't be influenced by the salesman's behavior, in which actions speak louder than words. Go after the best price you can get.

Last-Minute Fixups

You know, of course, the enormous importance of first impressions. Cars are no exception. In fact, they are likely to be judged on their superficial shine, cleanliness, and tidiness. They must *look* well cared for in order to persuade someone that they will work well, too.

So be smart. Whether or not you have consistently kept up your car's appearance, you will want to spruce it up as best you can for its showing.

Give your car a nice bath and then a good waxing. Polish all the chrome. If there are small nicks or abrasions on the finish, try to match the color with a tiny jar of car-finish paint made just for the purpose of touching up the surface here and there. Clean the windows until they are spotless and shimmering on both sides. Vacuum the upholstery and the rest of the interior so that no dog hairs or sand or dead leaves are to be found. Dust and polish the dashboard and doors. Scrub the tires, especially if they are white-walls, and make sure that the underside of the car looks clean—not covered with last winter's caked mud.

Obvious as these things may seem to some of you, they may not be at all obvious to others, who feel comfortable about letting things go. But here we are talking about more dollars for you, and if this is important, put some effort and elbow grease into fixing up your old car.

If you have a garage mechanic whom you trust, ask him to check over the car's engine and other functioning parts to determine what essential major repairs might be necessary that would be discerned by an outside expert. You want to be psychologically prepared for a less-than-anticipated price offer.

If you know that the tires have only a few thousand miles left in them, you can admit this to a potential buyer, and by discounting from the Blue Book price make a deal look more appealing and honest. Or you could consider buying a set of used but still tread-healthy tires from a junkyard or recycled car parts source.

If you are handy you can put in new hoses and belts to give the engine a well-tended look. (See Chapter 14 on taking care of your car for other ideas on a quick do-it-yourself fixup.) You can clean off the battery, carburetor, radiator, oil receptacle, and other parts to make everything look cleaner. You could even consider getting a steam cleaning under the hood.

How the New Car Market Affects Used Car Prices

Used car prices are very closely connected to the new car market. Usually they will go up when the new car sales are slow. This is because fewer used cars are being traded in; therefore they are scarcer. Demand for available used cars increases, driving up the prices.

If you are driving a used car that is clean and in good working order, it is wise for you to buy your new car when new car sales are slow. In this way you can take advantage of the premium price your used car will bring if you trade it or decide to sell it privately. Because of the sluggishness of the new car market, you're apt to get a better deal from a sales-hungry dealership.

WARNING: If there is a hot period of new car sales, used cars will hold their value until the appetite of the used car buyers is satisfied. Once the immediate heavy demand for used cars is met, a glut of used cars is possible. The value of your trade-in can rise or fall quickly. I gave another example in Chapter 10: How a disaster, such as a flood, can increase the value of your used car overnight by as much as $2,000 and then drop quickly a few weeks afterward.

A strong reminder: When new car sales are slow, *all* used cars are in high demand.

How to Place a Value on Your Car

So what is your car worth? When everything works properly, you can take the guessing away from the used car appraiser.

The prices in the classified section of your local newspaper will give you a general idea of the market or real value of particular used cars. These prices range between the standard wholesale and retail list prices.

Call a few of the numbers listed in the ads to find out what the seller tells you about the condition, including odometer reading, of his or her car and any willingness to bargain. Consult bankers and credit unions and wholesale-price guidebooks, such as states' Blue Books, to judge the fairness of the asking price.

If you are selling your car as a trade-in, make sure a generous-appearing figure is subtracted from the sum you negotiated with the salesman, *not* from the suggested retail price. Don't let the salesman distract you by getting you thinking back to sticker price and showing you a higher-price car.

And be aware of this: If you have had recent body damage, often a dealer or a used car salesman would rather have an insurance check than a repaired car. This check will be based on written estimates from several repair garages. You can point out in your negotiations that this is all it should cost to fix the car. Miscalculations could cost you several hundred dollars.

A chipped or cracked windshield, however, is one thing you absolutely should have fixed, or the cost of repairing it will be deducted. People—even the professionals—are simply put off by an unpleasant- or unsafe-looking windshield. Good insurance will usually provide windowglass damage coverage, so getting this taken care of—even though it will cost you whatever your deductible is on your insurance—should earn you an extra $200 for the car.

Every dealer and used car salesman is looking for a used car that can be put on the front line of the lot after a detail cleanup and a minor safety and maintenance check. If you did not take care of your old car, you now realize that it will pay you to take care of your next one!

Determining the Wholesale and Retail Prices

This is tricky terrain. I have been at management meetings with as many as 150 sales managers from similar dealerships in similar areas. Two or three used cars of the types these men sell would be displayed and the sales managers would be asked to appraise their dollar values.

One would think that these men would more or less make the same appraisals. Actually, their appraisals varied as much as $1,500 between low and high estimates. The real professionals gave estimates in the middle of this range.

What are some of the reasons for such wild differences in evaluating used cars? The highs and lows are usually from managers who:

• Don't know if a particular car is popular or unpopular in their area.
• Have a buyer for one like it already.
• Have three just like it on their lot now.
• Have just sold one like it.
• Have little interest in used cars. (In such a dealership the dealer should hire a used car manager rather than leave these estimates to an uninterested new car manager.)

Oddly enough, some dealers in a given market cannot sell a specific clean, used car at any reasonable price, even though they offer the car to a retail buyer at hundreds of dollars below the competition. They may eventually wholesale the car to a used car wholesaler or to a dealer who handles that make. Ironically, the dealer to whom it is wholesaled may price it higher than the original dealer—and still sell it!

Just as each dealership has its own personality, the same is true of used car lots. Certain cars will sell well on one dealer's lot and not on another's. These distinctive personalities are developed by experience, selection, merchandising, and marketing. You might find real bargains at a dealership handling cars inappropriate to its kind of business.

Should You Sell to a Dealer or to a Private Party?

Your car is very special to you whether it has 5,000 or 150,000 miles on it. You probably feel overly possessive, even though you may not have had it very long.

But no matter how precious it is, your car is a used car at the time of trade-in, and the dealer must view it as such. The private buyer also knows it's a used car. Both the dealer and the individual buyer want your used car for the lowest price you are willing to accept. They may not treat your sentiments about your car very tenderly.

Both dealer and private buyer might use any means they can to persuade you to accept their offer. Some of these methods will be quite obvious to you, whether they are highly positive—gushing compliments and appealing to your emotions—or downright negative and unpleasant, such as high pressure, intimidation, or making you feel stupid or embarrassed. Other techniques are intended to make you lower your guard and agree to an unfair price.

It's vital to realize that when you sell or trade in your car, you are switching from the buyer's to the seller's role, and you'll want to get the best price you can. So try to use some of the closing techniques that a dealership's salesman would use in selling you a car. It will be good experience!

If you can't get the right price for your trade-in, consider: (1) looking for other buyers; (2) keeping the car yourself; or (3) caving in to the dealer's offer.

But don't dismiss too quickly your car's first potential buyer, whether a dealer or a private party. Many times that offer turns out to be the best deal.

Shopping for Trade-in Values

After determining the price of the car you want, it might be to your advantage to comparison shop if you don't like the trade-in allowance. If you are following the directions I gave earlier, you already know how much the new car will cost *without* your trade-in. Actually, that's one major reason why I advised you earlier not to mention your trade-in at all—if you can manage this rather tricky maneuver—*until* you have a firm price on the vehicle of your choice. This is not being underhanded, because you probably don't know yet if you will trade, sell, or keep. The final decision should be determined by what solution offers you the best deal.

However, if the new car quotation was based on your turning in your present car as a trade-in, ask the dealer what that price would be *without* a trade-in. Then shop to see whether you can sell the trade-in on your own at a better price.

Drive your old car to as many dealerships as you like and ask to see the used car sales managers. Ask straight out how much they'd pay for your car. Remember that they will try to sell you a car, new or used, to replace the one you want to sell them!

Information on Your Trade-in

Whether you intend to trade in your car or not, most dealers will refer to it as "your trade-in." By knowing their interests ahead of time, you can use them to your own advantage.

Smart dealers train their salesmen to politely discuss general information with you. Their questions are good ones. Anticipate them before you talk business with the dealer. Plan your answers.

Smart dealers also have the authorized used car appraiser fill out a form giving his opinions of what your present car is worth. Here are some sample questions, some others you should ask yourself, and a professional used car checklist.

Determining the Wholesale and Retail Prices
Your Personal Information Sheet

• What kind of car are you driving? _____
brand name

_____   _____   _____ _____
Year   model or style   2-door   4-door

• Are you going to trade in your car or truck on this purchase?

                               _____ _____
Yes   No

• If so, how do you intend to advertise it for sale?

_____ _____ _____ _____
word of mouth bulletin board newspaper or radio ad other

• If you are not trading in, do you intend to keep your old car?

                               _____ _____
Yes   No

• If none of the above options apply, what do you intend to do?

_____

• How much is your car or truck worth? _____
• On what do you base this judgment? _____
• If you sell the car or truck yourself, which of these items below apply?:

_____ Buyer will pay cash.
_____ Buyer will finance it.

_____ Buyer will finance it with my help.
_____ Buyer will make payments to me.
_____ I intend to guarantee the car or truck for _____ months.

Trade-in Checklist

Insert a dollar value in the + or − column if you can ascertain it. If a dollar value is not appropriate, insert "Okay," "Needs repair," or whatever comment is appropriate.

Model and/or Item	(a) good Condition/pluses	(b) bad Condition/minuses
2-door	+ $	
4-door	+ $	
Wagon	+ $	
Other	+ $	
Color	+ $	− $
Exterior condition	+ $	− $
Interior condition		− $
Tires	+ $	− $
Glass		− $
Body		− $
Odometer (high, low)	+ $	− $
Carpeting		− $
Seats		− $
Engine—4,6,8 cylinder	+ $	− $
Transmission—3,4,5, auto	+ $	− $
Power steering	+ $	− $
Power brakes	+ $	− $
Air conditioning	+ $	− $
Vinyl top	+ $	− $
Radio (type)	+ $	− $
50/50 seats	+ $	
Custom interior	+ $	
Custom exterior	+ $	
Power seats	+ $	− $

Model and/or Item	(a) good Condition/pluses	(b) bad Condition/minuses
Power windows	+ $	− $
Power door locks	+ $	
Tilt steering wheel	+ $	
Cruise control	+ $	
TOTAL	+ $	− $
	a minus b	
ACTUAL VALUE		

Disadvantages of Selling Privately

Consider the possible negative aspects of selling your car to a private party:

1. You're stuck at home to answer the phone and show the car.
2. If you work or go away, you may have to impose on a family member or friend to stay at your house to answer the telephone or wait for people who want to see your car.
3. People call you at irregular hours.
4. The possibility of an uninsured accident while a potential customer is test driving your car.
5. Your car might be stolen by someone allowed to test drive it. Cars have been known to vanish forever. A ring of professional thieves can disassemble a car in a matter of minutes and sell the parts to unsuspecting body shops or salvage yards that have customers waiting for them.
6. Having to negotiate the sale of your car.
7. Having problems later should anything go wrong with your ex-car.
8. The legal responsibility connected with selling a car.
9. The possible inconvenience of having to meet the buyer at the bank to collect your money, sign over your title, etc.

A title and car registration are legal ownership papers. In some states the buyer has the responsibility of obtaining them. You must receive one or both when you buy a car, and if you are selling you must furnish a buyer with the same.

Responsibility regarding the title or ownership transfer varies from state to state. California law regarding title transfer requires the seller to mail a copy of the sales transaction so that the Department of Motor Vehicles can collect all the sales tax due. Many states, however, have no such requirement.

Beware of Odometer Laws

Did you buy your present trade-in when it was new? More importantly, can you guarantee the mileage on the odometer?

Then ask yourself: Was the odometer broken for any period of time? Have you ever driven the car with the odometer disconnected? Did you change the odometer? Did you ever turn the mileage back or have it turned back?

If you answer no to either of the first two questions or yes to any of the next four, you may well have problems if you have not cleared up the matter before you sell your car. Federal laws prohibit you from misrepresenting your car's mileage. Such activities are punishable by a $10,000 fine and/or a jail sentence. You must inform the buyer in writing of problems with the odometer, including any history of its having been out of order.

Therefore, if *you* purchase a used car, make sure you receive a mileage disclosure statement, signed by the seller, before the title is transferred.

In Wisconsin, a person who has been sold a used car with an odometer that was tampered with can recover from the car seller $1,500 or three times the amount of the damages, whichever is greater. The law also declares that if you sell a vehicle and either knowingly or unknowingly guarantee the mileage and later it is proven to be different, you must buy back the car or truck at the price paid to you, or else you can be taken to court.

Other states have similar laws. For more information about your own state, contact the state attorney general's office.

Federal law might someday require each state to have a space on the ownership title of a car for insertion of the odometer mileage or other important information regarding the speedometer as well as leasing, rental, police usage, or flood damage. This information would be inserted at the time of title transfer by the seller, to be recorded permanently on the front of the title. It would effectively prevent odometer tampering and other unethical and deceitful acts by car sellers.

Auto dealers can purchase odometer insurance. Many of them do this as a sensible protection for their business, which cannot easily absorb fines. Private car sellers get no such insurance and are in a far more vulnerable position.

If you purchased your car new and are absolutely sure the mileage is accurate, you are safe. If it was purchased used, either you or an interested prospective buyer could trace its history back to the original owner to be sure that the odometer reading is correct. I cannot overemphasize the importance of this.

In 1984 the State of Wisconsin investigated over 13,000 cars that had come in from out-of-state dealers. They were suspected of having altered titles, altered odometers, or switched serial numbers. This was being done because Wisconsin is one of the few states that guarantee a car title to be good. One automobile dealer had been warned not to buy used cars from certain used car wholesalers, but he continued to do this. He was severely reprimanded by the State of Wisconsin, and his business then came under close official scrutiny.

WARNING: If you did not purchase your car or truck new from a dealership, or if it was purchased privately and you are not absolutely sure of the mileage, when you sign your agreement DO NOT CHECK the area that binds you to guarantee the odometer mileage.

Selling Your Own Car

Goods are advertised to get attention, to tell what you want to sell, and to call for action from potential buyers and let them know where you are.

One individual can't afford elaborate advertising to sell one car. However, study the ways dealerships use words to attract buyers. Vary their themes to suit your own purposes.

Unless you have succeeded with word of mouth and found a buyer willing to pay a fair price for your car, you must advertise to let people know that your car is for sale. One good way is to post small notices on bulletin boards in such places as supermarkets and college campuses (don't forget to include your phone number). You can also put up a For Sale sign, again including your phone number and briefly stated details, on a window of the car so that it will be noticed by passing drivers and pedestrians.

Also keep in mind company, church, and organization newsletters that are willing to carry brief notices; service stations and car repair garages that may be willing to alert customers that you want to sell your car; and special car-trading programs on the radio.

Newspaper advertising is swifter and more efficient. It will cost money (but not a great deal) to run a small classified ad. You get a special rate if you run the ad for more than one day.

To get an idea of how best to compose your ad, look at automobile ads in the classified advertising sections of local newspapers. Ads that appeal to you might well appeal to others. Also look at prices of cars similar to yours.

Surefire Zingers

Many dealers use certain zingers or "buzz" expressions to make the cars on their lots sound appealing to would-be buyers. If you decide to advertise your car, try some of them out, with your own variations. You'll like the results you get.

- Must Sell . . .
- Here's an exciting . . .
- Take a look now at . . .
- Picture yourself in . . .
- Now we'd like to show you . . .
- A real savings comes with . . .
- A smart buyer will like . . .
- You've heard of the cream puff—here's a . . .
- A car for the family . . .
- You'll be proud to drive . . .
- Low-low payments on this . . .
- Look no more, here's . . .
- A car price you can afford . . .
- Any reasonable offer considered . . .

How to Advertise if You Decide to Sell Your Car

Here are a few examples of classified ads to give you a general idea of how they should be written:

- Settling estate—must sell—1986 Lincoln Custom Sedan 3,000 miles, with every option, was $24,000 new, sky pink, custom, crushed earth green interior, sunroof, split front seats, only asking $17,900. Call 1-222-222-2222, between 6 and 9 P.M.
- 1985 Cadillac Eldorado, 15,000 miles, this beautiful machine has leather seats and all the other luxury features you have always wanted. Just received company car so any reasonable offer over

$19,000 considered—HURRY! Call 1-222-222-2222—9 A.M. to 6 P.M.

- Must sell—1983 Chrysler—a lot of miles left on this beauty— jet black, loaded with all the toys, including sunroof and split seats—you'll drool when you see it. First $6,500 owns it. Call 1-222-222-2222, Saturday 9 A.M. to 5 P.M.
- 1982 AMC—good running transportation with a lot of miles left, like new. Any reasonable offer considered, asking $3,800. Call 1-222-222-2222, until 9 P.M.
- 1974 Station Wagon—good for hunting, fishing, or camping. Needs some body work. $399. Call 1-222-222-2222 weekdays.

Using Common Sense in Selling Your Car

Always remember to protect yourself as much as possible when running a newspaper ad or posting notices. You never know who might answer your ads, so be prepared. Use the following common-sense guidelines when selling your car privately.

1. When advertising your car for sale, always keep a pen and pad by the phone. Be like a salesman: First ask for the caller's phone number, write it down, and then have the caller repeat the number. Ask his or her name, write that down (asking how it is spelled), and get his or her full address. Also ask for the business phone.

2. Don't let a person come to your home if he or she won't give you in advance his or her name, address, and phone number(s). Get that information first; then call back to make the appointment. This way, you can make sure that you have been given a correct phone number, and you have a means of tracing the person if something goes awry.

3. Don't let anyone enter your home who looks suspicious or makes you feel uncomfortable. Trust your instincts. The same holds true for letting this person drive your car, either with you or alone.

4. Before you let anyone drive your car, ask to see his or her driver's license and make some notes from it, including the license number.

5. Do not sign over your title or give your car to anyone until all purchasing arrangements have been made.

6. Finally, have the person bring cash, a certified check, or a cashier's check. If you are given a personal check, wait for it to clear the bank before you turn over the title to the car. (In the meantime, of course, you will have supplied the buyer with a proper receipt of purchase, noting that the delivery of the car and title are contingent upon the check's proving good.) WARNING: Beware of bogus certified checks. Unless you are totally familiar with the buyer of your car, go to the bank that issued the check and see if it is good. Some areas of the country, particularly New York, have a problem with phony certified stamps being used on checks by unscrupulous people.

7. If you still owe money on your car, you will have to settle with the lending institution. If the person who buys your car is assuming your payments, go to the lending institution with him or her to make sure that such an arrangement is permitted and that you will be free of future responsibility in case of default.

Saying Goodbye to an Old Friend

So you have finally sold your car.

It is time now to bid farewell to "Friend Flicka," or whatever name you've given it. You have traveled over many roads together, building up miles and memories and sharing happiness, adventure, disappointments, thrills, and perhaps a few spills.

You have taken good care of each other in a mutually beneficial service. And all the while the two of you have helped family and friends, even some strangers.

There is bound to be strong sentiment between you two, in spite of some inevitable tensions and tussles through the years.

But now, almost as if you're both changing jobs and homes and moving to separate states, the hour for aloha-saying has arrived. Reminisce for a while. And then pat your old friend on its warm metallic back—before you both drive away to new friends and associations.

TWELVE

How About Leasing?

Tennessee's Elvis Blalock, a restaurant-chain owner, was vocal about his dislike for buying a car every two years. Lend-Lease Bertha, overhearing his conversation, spoke out, enthused about the options and advantages of the "wonderful world of car leasing."

"Where have you been all these years, when I've really needed you?" asked Elvis. "Why didn't anyone tell me *before* about car leasing? Just how long has it been going on?"

"Since the fifties," Bertha told him. "And nowadays about twenty-five percent of all cars sold will be leased to businesspeople and to businesses like yours."

"Where do I sign?" Elvis implored her. "And how soon can you get me the largest and fanciest car they make?"

Elvis—who liked and maybe needed high visibility in his community—settled for a Hong Kong Golden Arrow. Excited that the use of this elegant vehicle would cost only $2,000 a month, he went for an open-end lease for two years.

After driving the limousine for six months, Elvis decided he didn't really like his dream car after all. "It isn't all they brag it up to be," he concluded.

Elvis drove over to Bertha's car-leasing agency and explained his problems to her. "Vandals have scratched it up and cut the top, almost as if they were trying to *kill* the car," he said. "I have to keep it in my garage most of the time just to protect it. If I go anywhere, I've got to park it where I can keep my eye on it every second. But I leased it just so I could have *fun!*. . .Bertha, you can take it back right now."

Bertha reached in a file drawer, pulled out the agreement, and quietly read all Elvis's contractual obligations to him. "Mr. Blalock," she said, "you are responsible for the balance due on the car. You can sell the car, we can sell it, or you can find a person who can take over your payments if he's judged worthy by our financial institution. However, you are still responsible for the conditions in the lease agreement itself, such as any amount due above the actual wholesale value established at the expiration of the lease. And the damage to the car that you have described will detract from its value."

Elvis looked at Bertha in shocked disbelief. "Why, this is no different, really, than *owning* a car. Except that my company gets to write off the lease payment on our income taxes. Meanwhile, I'm paying your company a fee of two thousand dollars a month. And I'll bet a big chunk of that goes for your own overhead and profit."

Bertha just smiled at him politely. "It's all in our standard contract," she said. "Nobody hid anything from you."

Elvis kept his Golden Arrow. It's still parked in his garage. Occasionally he drives it around, but he tries to stick close to the best neighborhoods, where there's less chance of resentment toward opulence. Humbly, he takes in all the comments: "My, what a splendid car you have." . . . "Isn't it a joy to be so rich." . . . "Now, *that's* traveling in style!"

"I'm going back to buying cars," he now says. "Next time."

Just as there is more than one way to skin a cat, there is more than one way to have a new car at your disposal. While buying a car is by far the most widely known and accepted way, leasing the car is an alternative—and sometimes the better alternative. Leasing is increasingly done these days, particularly for business purposes, as it has decided tax advantages. Statistics, if one can believe them, indicate that more than a quarter of the vehicles on the road are leased.

Shall I keep my Cadillac, Lincoln, Rolls-Royce, or Mercedes?

When Should You Lease?

Leasing is an answer for some people some of the time. It can be a good idea when you don't want to tie up your working capital. There is no down payment—the customary security deposit is actually the first and last lease payment paid in advance. Leasing also does not affect your line of credit. However, your credit still has to be good to lease a car—at least as good as it would have to be to buy a new car.

For small businesses where the proprietor cannot afford to maintain both a work and a personal car, leasing can offer a sensible solution.

If you are in a high-income tax bracket, leasing may work out better than buying a car. Your accountant or tax consultant should be able to tell you if it would be smart financially.

Whenever the cost of money is extremely high, however, you should think things through carefully. You might be able to purchase a new car outright and finance the loan at a much lower rate of interest than the rate charged by the leasing company.

Where Can You Lease?

Some of the national automobile leasing companies are McCullagh, Peterson, Howell & Heather, and Gelco. In addition, Hertz, Avis, National, and Budget lease cars on a long-term basis. Check the Yellow Pages to find out where leased cars are available near you—you should find at least several outlets in your area. You can do preliminary checking by phone on their charges.

Leasing of cars is also done at nearly every auto dealership. A dealer can have as few as ten cars on lease. However, 500 to 800 cars out on lease can be a manageable and very profitable portion of a dealership business.

Some leasing companies have lost large sums because of a driver's bad driving habits. This is why smart dealers conduct a complete credit and character check on you if you want to lease. The rule of thumb is, "If the person couldn't buy a car, don't lease to him either." And in this case the dealer, because he legally owns the car, really takes the large risk with damage and accidents.

Many leasing operations can make a bundle if they are well run.

The high rate of inflation in the 1970s and early '80s made leasing an especially profitable operation for dealers. But it has become very important for dealers to calculate accurately the ultimate resale value of a leased car. High inflation created many increases in the price of new cars and many jumps in the value of used cars.

How Leasing Works

HOW TO ESTIMATE RATES

A lease payment is computed in different ways. One way is to figure the value of the leased car at the end of the lease—say, three years—by taking the price from a current used car wholesale book to determine the value of a similar car that is now three years old.

Another way to calculate the monthly lease payment is to depreciate the car 2 percent per month from the price paid for it. Suppose, for example, that a car is purchased for $10,000.

Cost of car $10,000
Depreciation rate × .02
Depreciation each month $200

Cost of car $10,000
Interest each month × .01
Interest each month $100

Overhead ($10 to $30, usually $20) $20
Profit ($10 to $50, usually $20) $20

Total proposed price per month for leased car: $340

THE LEASE TERM

As a general rule, the shorter the lease period, the higher the monthly rate; the longer the lease period, the lower the monthly rate. This reflects the fact that the rate of depreciation on a new car is the highest in the first year and then sinks gradually with each successive year. Since the dealer ultimately wants to sell the cars he leases, he cannot afford to let them get too old or be driven too many miles, or he will be unable to get a good resale price on them. So the length of the lease, the miles driven, and the anticipated condition of the leased car all figure into the dollar amount of the lease payment and estimated value of the car at the end of the lease.

INSURANCE

Anyone who has his name on a car title thereby acknowledges ownership and is responsible for its insurance. This is no different for the owner of cars for lease than it is for any other kind of car. If you are leasing a car, it is wise to check on your dealer's insurance and be sure you are given the proper identification papers to take with you. But you will find, in general, that all dealerships handling lease fleets are eager to protect their investments. Just make certain you have insurance on the car—your insurance and/or theirs. If you carry your own insurance, your payments should be lower, unless your insurance covers less than the dealer's normal policy.

CLOSED- AND OPEN-END LEASING

Closed-end leasing means that you owe nothing at the end of the lease period other than the cost of repairing any unusual damage to the car, or the cost for any additional miles you have driven over the number of miles agreed upon in the lease.

Open-end leasing means that you must guarantee the value of the car at the end of the lease period. This value is calculated at the time of the contract signing.

Your payments could be lower on an open-end lease, but you should be aware that this type of lease could prove more expensive in the long run. In an open-end lease, you guarantee the wholesale value of the car; but the payment can be made lower by the leasing company, to show a higher resale value than is realistic at the end of the lease—which will give the lessee lower payments but means the lessee might not be in good financial condition to pay the difference between actual value and guaranteed value at the end of the lease. Many states have laws protecting you, the lessee, so that you cannot be held liable for more than three months of payments if the residual value of the vehicle is too low.

An open-end lease also sometimes creates an income tax reporting problem. The Internal Revenue Service has declared open-end leases to be conditional sales contracts. The lessee gets the tax break—making this a subject of dispute with the car-leasing companies.

Don't go into leasing blindfolded. Keep your eyes open and read the contract carefully. If you do lease and your choice is open-ended, make sure you have *in writing* the option to buy the car at the end of the lease period for a guaranteed price—the residual value or dollar amount you are guaranteeing the car to be worth at that time.

TERMINATION OF LEASE

The conditions under which the dealer may terminate the lease are listed in the default clause of the leasing contract. Read this section of the contract very carefully. There are, however, a number of different types of leasing contracts. So even if you have leased before, you certainly should read yours to be aware of any special provision. Something may be different about it—something you will need to know about.

Because an open-end lease is actually considered a finance contract, in essence you own the car. With a closed-end contract the penalty for an early termination is different. Ask questions and read the contract section covering this. Ask to have the terms spelled out clearly so you know, up front, your obligation if you must terminate leasing early for some reason.

When you lease a car, the same as when you buy one, cut the best deal you can.

A Leasing Checklist

Here are a few things that you, as a lessee, should make sure are included in any car-leasing agreement:

- An accurate description of both lessee and lessor.
- Detailed description of the vehicle and extra equipment.
- Complete details of all terms and conditions, including the monthly rental and all other particulars on which the lessee and lessor have agreed.
- Spaces for signatures of the parties and witnesses.

Among the details that should be included in the particulars to which the lessor and lessee agree are:

1. Amount of damage deposit, if any, and whether rental is to be paid a month in advance (which is normal).
2. Exact rental charge, how it is to be prorated over the first month or part of month, and whether there will be an additional fee for excess mileage over an agreed-upon monthly amount.
3. Which party is responsible for such expenses as taxes, licensing fee, titling, and registration. All state, county, and local charges and assessments should be accounted for, so that nothing is left to create misunderstandings later.
4. Ownership, though obvious, should be spelled out as the lessor's, with the lessee's acknowledging in writing that he has rights only to the use of the vehicle for the specified period.
5. The extent to which both the lessor and the lessee are responsible for damages within and beyond their controls should be stated. If the insurance has a deductible clause, that should be specified, as should the party responsible for covering that amount in the event of an accident or other loss.
6. Any other insurance matters as required by the insurer.
7. Indemnification of the lessor by the lessee for any liability the lessee incurs, beyond the control of the lessor, while operating the vehicle.
8. A default clause, usually quite lengthy, that specifies the reasons for which the lessor can reclaim the vehicle if the lessee does not pay the rental, does not live up to other terms of the lease, loses his credit rating, or becomes unsatisfactory in other specified ways.
9. Maintenance arrangements specifying who is responsible for taking care of what and on what schedule.
10. Anything else deemed necessary for the parties to include in order to solidify the agreement and avoid future misunderstandings.

Maintenance

Because as lessee you must guarantee the car's value at turn-in time or pay for any repairs on damage to the car, you probably would want to take even better care of a leased car than of your own car. This could certainly be done easily with cosmetic items: tending to the exterior by washing, waxing, and retouching small nicks, and keeping the interior clean as well as mending any small tears in upholstery.

NOTES:

You're the service manager? You look like a medicine man . . . please tell me where my car hurts.

THIRTEEN

Getting the Services
Your Car Needs

Prudence Patience's fairly new car had been in the Portland dealer's service department for nine days. The automatic transmission had been leaking fluid and wasn't shifting right. This was the third time in three weeks she had brought it in with the same complaint, and her car was yet to be properly fixed. Now she needed it in perfect shape for her long-planned vacation trip.

She called the service writer at noon on Friday to find out what time she could pick up her car. "What do your keys look like?" he asked her. "We can't find them."

"Do you mean to tell me that you haven't even *begun* to work on my car?" Prudence said, with a trace of irritation in her voice. She described her keys, which were found at once hanging on a nearby pegboard.

"Good," the service manager told her. "We'll get started on your car on Monday morning."

This was the last straw for Prudence Patience. "I am *leaving* on my vacation on Monday morning," she said, "and I'm taking my repaired car with me. You've already had a week and a half to fix it, and you couldn't even call me to say you'd misplaced the keys! What kind of place are you running there, anyway?"

Furious, she phoned the sales manager and then the dealer himself to lodge her complaints. Prudence, who had never threatened anyone before, was seeing red. "See that my car gets fixed *today,* or I'm going to use the lemon law against you people."

By midafternoon her irate phone calls had gotten results. The service manager arranged for a mechanic to come in and work at overtime wages all weekend, if need be, to get her car readied for her by early Monday morning.

Prudence was learning that, past a certain point, patience is not necessarily a virtue.

When you take your car home to stay, you're hoping that it will be all that you wish it to be and do everything you want it to, without ever causing you a moment of trouble.

But of course that's unrealistic. Sooner or later, no matter how well you treat it, you and your car are bound to encounter problems. Time and stress take a toll on the best of mechanisms.

Dealing with Car Service Personnel

Unless you come into the dealership to visit with your salesman, kick tires, bring someone in to buy a car, or just make a quick stop to buy parts, your time there will be spent in the customer lounge, service department, or body shop.

When you need service, it's not absolutely necessary to take your automobile back to the dealership from which you purchased it. But it is a wise decision if the dealership is conveniently located and proves to be well run. This dealership should be interested in making you happy and retaining your good will. By saying pleasant things about them and the car they sold you, you are giving them the least expensive and most effective means of advertising any business could hope for.

Service representatives of the dealership assume that customers come in for any of the following reasons:

- For help on some automotive-related issue, such as recalls or service policies.
- Because they have car problems.
- To get free information about their car.
- To visit with their favorite mechanic.

There's a dealer 100 miles south of here.

There are three rules for customers in dealing with car service departments:

1. Be pleasant.
2. Be considerate.
3. Clearly state the problem(s) with your car.

All dealership employees and garage repair mechanics are human beings, just like you and me. Perhaps they too have a spouse and hungry mouths at home to feed—maybe two or three children, a parakeet, dog, cat, and goldfish; plus a house mortgage, house installments, and even car payments.

Most service departments at dealerships or car repair garages work the conventional five-day week, but some work extended hours in order to accommodate customers.

Many people make it a high priority to show up on time for an appointment with the service department, eager to discuss whatever car problems they have with the service manager. Others, however, do not seem to understand that their casualness about timing can cause real hardships for service personnel, particularly in very busy places or at peak hours when scheduling conferences and repairs is a tight matter indeed. Such disregard will not be appreciated, and might very well result in unsatisfactory relations with the people who are expected to fix up a car in trouble.

Problems that Warranties Should Cover

Years ago, under a warranty, carburetors might require as many as five or six trips to a service department. The repair procedure was to replace one item at a time. Sometimes they were totally fixed the first time, but many times it meant a number of trips. Then pollution controls made it increasingly more difficult to repair carburetors. Finally, the unit was sealed so that now, if a problem appears, the whole carburetor is replaced.

A similar thing happened with one of General Motors' engines. If something went wrong, the entire engine was replaced. G.M. wanted the removed engine untampered with, so that their engineers could personally examine it piece by piece to discover the probable weakness or cause of failure. Now, that's progress!

The same procedure was used on a transmission by a domestic manufacturer when a pattern of problems began to develop. This process doesn't inconvenience the customer and perhaps can get to the root of the problem quickly by determining whether a part is defective only in isolated instances or else is somehow predisposed to fail in many cars of that particular model.

Manufacturers' Recalls of Defective Cars and Car Parts

When the manufacturer discovers a consistent factory engineering malfunction, the recall starts.

The strongest emphasis is always on safety-related problems. They are usually detected by consistent customer complaints in warranty claims submitted by the dealer to the factory.

Once the computer picks up a pattern of reports on a particular failure, it alerts the factory that a problem exists. When a defect is discovered, people owning similar cars with like equipment are contacted.

The factory knows when the production date problem began and when it ended. They generally contact a few thousand owners with serial numbers prior to and after the onset of the problem. The public believes that the factory does not like recalls because they are costly, but in fact many people buy additional parts and service, or even a new car.

A recall generally has no limitation on time or mileage or number of owners.

WARNING: Never ignore a factory recall. The consequences could be serious.

But I wonder how many car buyers stopped buying American cars because of apparent service problems, misunderstandings, or misdiagnoses in the past years. It never helps when dealerships fail to be sympathetic toward new car owners with problems.

In most past instances, if something was not in Chevrolet's warranty Flat Rate Manual, a dealer had to have the work approved by someone in the zone service department. If this was not done, the dealer would not be paid by Chevrolet for the work. The other manufacturers had their individual policies, but were essentially the same.

Some years ago the Charleston, West Virginia, zone had a zone service manager who was impossible regarding customer service. His attitude was, "If it's in the book, okay; if not, NO!" I called him many times about legitimate customer complaints which Chevrolet should have approved. The answer was almost always a flat and emphatic "NO!"

Perhaps he was only following company policy, but after he was asked to leave Chevrolet, his replacement's attitude was 180 degrees different. He listened, considered the problem, and used common sense. While we didn't always agree with him, he always made fair, sensible decisions. The new manager's manner, and the philosophy that went with it, made it much easier for a dealership to satisfy its customers.

Times have changed too. I know the following is the current policy of both domestic and import manufacturers: satisfy current customers, win back past customers, and try to gain new customers. Today manufacturers are making sincere attempts to solve and satisfy all complaints. Dealers, as the local representatives of manufacturers, are paying better attention to customers and will continue to do so.

The "mooch"—that customer who is trying to get what he doesn't deserve—may unfortunately get his way more often nowadays. But as the old saying goes, "It's the squeaking wheel that gets the oil."

The improved relations between dealers and customers make up for these rare cases of exploitation.

Warranty Problems

Every buyer of a new car and many buyers of used cars have warranties that guarantee certain replacements of parts and even some labor. All of these warranties read differently, and all too often they are written in such a way, using lawyers' jargon, that their meanings are difficult to fathom. Once the customer has read and, with luck, understood the warranty, the next problem often becomes how to collect on the promises therein if the need arises.

How to Proceed When Something Goes Wrong

If your car is not behaving right, first schedule a diagnostic procedure and arrange a convenient service appointment. When it is time for the car actually to be repaired, the service writer will write up the repair order (R.O.). This order, with carbon copies, is given to the parts department. This enables them to order any extra parts necessary for the repair.

A hard copy of the R.O. is given to the head mechanic, who decides how his team of mechanics will handle the job. This hard copy is a permanent record of all parts installed and all labor done on the car. In a modern dealership, this information may be stored in the computer, with the information about your car available to the service writer. No parts are released to the mechanic without the R.O. The parts are recorded on the copies in the parts department so that someone pays for them—either the customer, the factory under warranty, the mechanical-breakdown insurance, or the dealership if the problem was their responsibility.

Stating the Problem Clearly

Service department managers repeat this story over and over. A customer calls and says that his car won't work. The service person asks if it turns over. The customer repeats that the car won't start. When the customer is asked if it cranks, he then asks what is meant by "cranks." The frustrated service person asks, "Does it go 'Umm, Umm' when the key is turned?" Sometimes it takes ten minutes to find out if the car engine turns over.

A whole bunch of customers line up at a dealership at 7 or 8 A.M., waiting to present the keys to their cars and talk about noises, rattles, and stalling problems. Many times they know nothing at all about basic auto mechanics. The service writer is stuck with a tough job, writing work orders based on vague information. Complaints are scarcely a firm basis for a diagnosis.

Here are some tips to help you communicate any problems to the service personnel about your car.

• First of all, it will help if you understand your car and cars in general. Familiarize yourself with the basic workings of automobiles by reading an article, say in an encyclopedia designed for easy reading. Study your car owner's manual. It is placed in the glove compartment of a new car, and for your convenience you should leave it there. Reading the manual carefully and following its instructions can prevent some problems. You will also learn a lot more about the car and its basic workings. No two people hear the same noise the same way, so insist on someone driving your car with you when you suspect a problem with the vehicle in motion.

• Be specific about the problem. Don't just call it "that noise in back," but explain what kind of noise it is, whether it is constant, exactly when it happens or is most noticeable (such as at high or low speeds or when increasing or decreasing speed), on which side it is located, and so on.

• With a problem such as stalling, take note of when it occurs. Only when the engine is hot or cold? When stopped at intersections? When making right or left turns? This will help narrow the possibilities of what the problem might be.

• If possible, have a service representative (perhaps even the person who is going to work on it) ride with you while you drive. You know your car and can identify and describe the problem better than a stranger can.

• If you suspect the problem may be hard to diagnose, do everybody a favor and stay away from the service department at 8 A.M. Generally that is their busiest time. Go in the middle of the afternoon, when it will be easier to get a service person to take a ride with you. You should also plan to leave your car there until the next day, so that they can have time with it.

• Ask to have any worn or damaged parts not covered by factory warranty saved for you when they are replaced. Then have them explain what went wrong and tell you what they did to correct the problem. Act as if you know what they are talking about, and be a good listener. You can throw out the old parts when you get home, or have them inspected for a second opinion. They don't know who might inspect the parts and the work after you leave with your car. And keep your receipt. If you have a complaint later, you'll have backup evidence.

When You Meet with Indifference

A frequent customer complaint goes like this. You are alarmed by the unusual behavior of your car. It could be a rattle, squeak, tap, grind, whine, or groan. Or it may be a malfunction. For example, the air conditioner turns on by itself in midwinter, or the heater cannot be turned off in midsummer. Or it could be incredibly poor fuel economy in a car that was promised as fuel efficient.

But when you call or go into the dealership to talk to the service manager and start to describe the problem, his calm reaction is, "That's normal." You can hardly believe your ears.

By "normal" he means that the thing that bothers you falls within a normal range of tolerance for proper performance. But that response will hardly satisfy you when you believe you have a highly justifiable concern or complaint about a car for which you have paid a great deal of money, and for which you may also possess a warranty still in effect.

Either the service manager doesn't have any previous knowledge or real acquaintance with the nature of your complaint, or else he is lying to you, to cover up either his ignorance or an already known tendency of the equipment to malfunction in this way.

If the situation extends over a period of time and several visits, you begin to feel frustrated, disgusted, unhappy. You wonder if you have been stuck with a lemon *and* a bad dealer.

"Mr. Normal" is telling you that it is just too bad. And if a customer doesn't like it, all he can do is buy another car. This Mr. Normal, quite properly, ought to be fired! Someone in his position should be forthright and say "I know this problem is a source of irritation to you. We have not yet found a way to correct it, but we are working on eliminating this nuisance. Please keep in touch. We do not believe that your car is unsafe to drive. When we do come up with the solution, we will contact you."

Although it is the responsibility of the dealership to call you, call occasionally so that the service department keeps you and your problem in mind.

In addition, before you leave work or home to pick up your car at the shop, always call to make sure your car is ready. This practice can save you waiting time and extra trips.

Climbing the Chain of Command

If you have a problem with your new car and attempt to get it fixed at the dealership, you will first go to see the service writer, who is the frontline person in charge of determining the source and solution of the problem. If he isn't able to help you, see the service manager. And if he can't help you, you will have to go to the dealer himself. Then, if your visit with the chief meets with no success, go on to the local zone office. If they can't accommodate you, go up to the franchise's central office. If they can't or won't assist you with your problem, go to the national office, and if you are still not satisfied, contact the president of the company himself.

Always document your case in writing, and build up a whole file of papers, if necessary, in order to pursue your claim or grievance in a businesslike way. Include notes about conversations, whether in person or by phone, giving the date and time of day. Keep a copy for yourself and also send a copy to the person with whom you talked.

Manufacturers' or distributors' addresses are generally found in the back of your warranty book. If this isn't so, then ask for the name, address, and phone numbers of the local service representative, the manufacturer, or the distributor. If they will not tell you, call another dealership of the same make car in your city or another and they might gladly tell you, hoping to get you as a future client.

Again, to document your complaint, date it, put it in writing, and keep a copy for yourself. Send a similar letter, by certified mail, to "the office of the president"—be it a manufacturer or distributor.

However, if you do your job of communicating properly, your grievance will never go beyond the service department at the dealership. As a dealer's slogan goes: "If you don't have time to do it right the first time, how will you find time to do it right the second time—for nothing?"

It may turn out that you'll wind up right back at the dealership, dealing with the person with whom you first talked before this wild goose chase began. The best thing is to try to work out, without acrimony, a sensible solution that is agreeable to both you and the dealership.

How Mechanics Get Paid

In order to get along well in the world of cars, you should understand mechanics and how they operate.

A mechanic is not allowed to turn a wrench without an R.O. A few mechanics are paid a salary, or a combination of salary and hourly wage, with an incentive added. Some are paid the old-fashioned way: 40, 50, or 60 percent of the labor charge, along with minimum wage or an hourly wage for menial tasks. Most, however, are paid flat-hour wages, an indication of what fraction of an hour or hours a specific labor operation should require.

Manufacturers publish flat-rate manuals, establishing pay for work performed and parts installed under new car warranties. Some dealerships use only the manufacturer's manual. Others use an independent manual. Some use both. Each dealer has his own policy.

Keep in mind that the majority of mechanics are paid only when they actually *do* something. The dealership may have a customer labor rate of $32 per flat-rate hour. (This is the amount charged to you as a customer. The factory is generally charged approximately the same rate. The fixed-hour dollar rate paid to the mechanic might be $11.50 for each flat-rate hour performed.)

High technical work, such as that on the engine or transmission, may be classified as "A" work, paying the mechanic a higher hourly wage than "B," which in turn pays more than "C" and "D" labor.

If the flat-rate manual allots three hours to remove and replace brake shoes on Ed Fuller's car, and John the Mechanic completes the labor in one and a half hours, John is still paid for three hours of work. If John spends six hours on the same basic repair, he still gets paid for three hours—unless rotors and drums have to be turned, which adds to the labor operations and therefore pays more. It's all in the book.

So if you ask most mechanics to do something for *free,* they'll look at you as if you just fell out of a tree. Unless you have a real friendship with a mechanic, don't expect to charm him into taking precious time off to give you helpful advice or make some no-cost adjustment. Like most of us, they work for a living—and it isn't an easy one.

Judging a Service Department

You'll have made an initial judgment on a service department at a dealership *before* you purchased your new car there. Sometimes, though, this first impression may be overly positive. You will find this out when you start bringing your car in for warranty or periodic servicing.

Unfortunately, a number of disorganized service departments

have irresponsible mechanics cooling their heels while waiting for parts on your own rubber wheels. Or they start to work at 8:30 A.M. when they should have been under way by 7:30 or 8:00. When quitting time arrives, many are out the door with a bound, no matter how slow a start they had in the morning.

Then there's the widespread practice among professional mechanics of dispensing free advice. When asked by the head mechanic, public relations manager, sales manager, or even a customer, busy mechanics will drop what they are doing to look at a car's engine or listen to a peculiar sound. Every time he is interrupted, it makes it that much more difficult for him to remember where he left off, and that much easier to make mistakes, forget steps in a procedure, or cut corners.

These are several reasons why most successful dealerships, in accordance with OSHA (the federal Occupational Safety and Health Administration) and insurance law, do not allow customers in the service work areas. Also, customers can get hurt.

When mechanics are allowed to waste their time, it's ultimately expensive to everyone, including you. Therefore a forward-looking service department completes the work it was committed to do that day before anyone is allowed to go home. Discipline like this pays off with mechanics feeling responsible toward their work and their customers.

Get It in Writing

Most dealerships have discovered the hard way that the best service policy is to have any unusual or extraordinary repair requested through the head mechanic, who will check that any estimate is based on a thorough investigation of the car and *knowledge* of labor, parts, and overhead costs—not on a guess, even an "educated" one.

If the figure seems very high, the customer can then shop around to see whether the job can be done elsewhere at a lower base price. If the estimate proves much too low, the customer could later be angry that the service department led him astray by giving an unrealistic figure.

It is important to get the estimate *in writing*. This document should include a provision for the customer to be notified of unanticipated additional repairs and/or replacements, which require his permission for the go-ahead. Thus he may decide to withdraw from the completely scheduled repair if costs begin mounting too high.

Complaints about Poor Service

As an old saying has it, the auto business is the only business in which even a priest, a rabbi, or a preacher will lie to you. All the practices listed below have created distrust, anger, and bitterness among car dealers, auto companies, and customers.

A common customer complaint is that service departments are unable to deliver what some overzealous salesmen may have promised. In my experience, however, almost all customer complaints about poor service can be traced to one of the following areas:

1. Deception or downright lying; inept service advisers or mechanics.
2. Lack of common courtesy or concern on the part of service personnel.
3. Inability of the customer to explain adequately the car's problem.
4. Lack of up-to-date diagnostic equipment.
5. Failure of manufacturers to have parts on hand for recently introduced models.
6. Employees being rushed to finish a job in order to bring down labor costs.
7. Employees who take shortcuts.
8. Customers who are unwilling to pay for complete repairs but will settle for a "good enough" repair.
9. Customers' failure to follow company-recommended maintenance programs for the vehicle.
10. Defects caused by poor engineering.
11. Prescribing services not actually needed.
12. Unethical practices such as charging for warranty work not performed, or charging both the customer and the factory (under warranty) simultaneously.
13. Factory rebate programs not understood either by the factory or the dealer.
14. The "get him before he gets me" attitude by the factory, dealer, and customer.

Don't worry, pal—I'll take good care of you.

Service with a Smile

At a well-run dealership, the service manager handles each complaint with a smile and sincere concern. He should just listen until the customer has talked himself out and worked the excess adrenalin out of his system. A number of techniques can be used. For example, the service manager can speak more softly, which has the effect of making the customer lower his voice and speak more calmly. The aim is to get the customer settled down so that the problem can be discussed and dealt with.

A professional service adviser (writer) or manager is in a crucial position, and he should be the first person at the dealership the buyer talks to after a breakdown occurs.

The service department, many times referred to as "the back end," is probably the toughest department to manage in a dealership, but it doesn't have to be. The service manager and his people have to satisfy the customer, the employees, the dealer, and the manufacturer. In other words, the service manager is expected to satisfy *everyone*.

Ideally, the service manager should always be calm, collected, organized, eager to satisfy, and understanding; able to get all cars repaired on time; prepared to have all the necessary parts in stock; capable of working very closely with the parts department; committed to wait on each customer immediately; and confident of being all things to all people.

The late Paul Doucas, an Oldsmobile dealer in Milwaukee, had a followup customer service program. An employee would call and say, "I'm Mr. XXX and I'm calling for Mr. Doucas. Were you greeted promptly in our service department? Were you treated courteously? Was your car ready on time? Did we perform all the services you requested? What recommendations can you make to help us improve our services? We need your good will and value you as our customer."

As a result of such attentiveness, the Doucas service department was filled to capacity.

How to Make Your Complaints

If you are bothered about the quality of service or the manner in which it was done, or if the dealership has refused to remedy some problem that you believe should be covered by the warranty, make a complaint.

Know how your dealership's service department is organized. The person behind the counter is the service writer. The service manager is his boss. The next in line is the general manager, or acting manager in charge, and finally the dealer himself. If, after talking to all of them, you are still not satisfied, follow the procedures in your manual.

Even if you don't get satisfaction, somehow manage to be pleasant as you make the rounds in the chain of command with your grievance. Remember, when you verbally attack a service representative, the chances are that several other uninformed irate customers have just finished berating him. He isn't going to be terribly responsive to another volley of abuse.

If you politely say something like, "Pardon me, I really hate to bother you, but could you help me?" and do it with a pleasant smile, the service manager is apt to be far more agreeable. On the other hand, if you make things difficult for the mechanic or service representative, you'll only damage the likelihood of getting good service while you alienate the dealership employees. Even though their job is to serve you, some make *you* feel as if they're doing you a favor, and that you are actually bothering them by asking for help.

Problems with Employee Theft

It might give frustrated customers a better perspective to know that dealers must concern themselves with problems other than satisfying disgruntled car buyers.

Employee theft is a large problem for dealers. Indirectly, it also affects the customer, who may not only pay more for parts and services but also receive poorer service.

Some methods of employee theft take more imaginative forms than others. Dealers continually see cases in which office personnel manipulate the books or destroy paperwork to cover their dishonesty. Tremendous quantities of parts, materials, and tools—which can be used on outside jobs or resold and converted to cash—are often carried out of the workplace by employees.

There has been a great increase lately of collusion between

employees and their friends. Service work performed for employees' friends' vehicles are often not written up. Expensive inventory items are loaded into friends' cars.

Bodymen, lot boys, parts department employees, and managers also steal from dealerships. Nor are salesmen immune. Used car salesmen can pocket thousands of dollars per year in kickbacks received from customers or dealers to whom good deals were given.

A surprising number of sales managers, particularly used car managers, steal from dealers, and in various ways. They can collect cash from used car wholesalers for selling them a car at a price lower than the actual wholesale value of the car, receiving from, say, $25 to $800 on just one car. Or they can buy a used car and pay much more for it by check than the car's acknowledged worth, asking for some of the difference in cash given under the table. One dealer proved that $84,000 in checks had been written to his used car manager by various used car dealers. The manager was pocketing between $600 and $800 a week.

There are a variety of ways unethical used car managers can steal. At an auto auction, for instance, most payoffs are paid in cash and become the basis for a long-term relationship. Some sellers at auctions hold up two $100 bills saying, "These are for someone who pays my price." And his price might be a thousand dollars higher than actual wholesale value.

Just as many successful and savvy auto dealers have learned to use specialists in marketing, finance, and accounting, so too have they learned to use security specialists, particularly polygraph examiners. The main reason for using the polygraph is to protect the majority of truthful and honest employees. However, in today's business world employee theft is estimated at $20 to $50 billion annually. While some dealers use the polygraph to investigate such instances of possible dishonesty, others use polygraphs to conduct preemployment security clearance examinations.

Obviously, then, rampant employee theft is a problem that damages seller and buyer and service client. You would certainly earn a dealer's gratitude if you tell him privately of any incident in which you have proof, or even suspicion, that an employee of his may be stealing.

Getting Along with a Dealer

The most effective thing that you can say to a dealer is, "I purchased my car here because of the fine reputation you have. I have told my friends about what a nice place of business you have. I've been very happy here—*until now*. Would you please help me?"

A manager or dealer who really cares about attracting and keeping customers will *do* something, and soon, about recurring customer service troubles. He'll listen if you put it right, without attacking him personally. It is quite possible that what you say will be useful, if unwelcome, news to him. Don't go around complaining about your adverse experience somewhere unless you've fulfilled your obligation to report your dissatisfaction to that person best able to do something to change it.

For the good of your car and your own mental health, be nice but firm when asking to be helped. Always try to talk in a calm voice, not with anger. This way, you will always be treated like a special customer. If not, *then* get excited and demanding . . . and go through the chain of command.

But just keep those wheels moving. The next chapter will present a number of things you can do yourself to help them along.

FOURTEEN

Take Good Care of Your Car!

I'll-Do-It Irma did her own oil changes, lubrication, and other small jobs on her Silver Slipper, the fastest stock quarter-miler at the track. She even did engine tune-ups. And then Irma installed new brake pads and shoes on her car, without a hitch.

Irma was having trouble, though, with the transmission. It wasn't shifting to her liking, so she decided to tear it down. This was her first attempt at a major repair.

Irma's frustration grew as she tried to reassemble the transmission. "I have more parts than I started with," she said with exasperation. "And some of them just don't fit!" Irma's two-week vacation was entirely taken up with all this messing around with the transmission. In the process, she lost some parts and broke others.

Finally, disgusted with herself, she loaded all the scattered pieces in the trunk of the car, called the tow truck, and told its driver to haul her beloved Silver Slipper to its proper service garage, with its crew of professional mechanics.

"Well, you really did it this time, Irma, with your do-it-yourself-ing!" Gus scolded her. He'd have to charge her several hundred dollars just to put her transmission back into working order. "But you've got guts anyway, kid. Next time, stick to the small stuff."

All too late, I'll-Do-It Irma realized that her former triumphs had gone to her head. She simply wasn't up to the big things, like transmission repairs or engine overhauls. But because she was interested in learning, she hung around the garage and watched Gus put the complex mechanism back together and get it running smoothly again. She vowed, however, to restrain that impulse to fix *everything* herself.

It's smart to keep your car in good shape. It will stay closer to its original value if you make sure that it not only looks attractive but also is in excellent working order.

You know how it is, don't you? If you let something go unrepaired for a while, you are inviting worse trouble.

Keeping something up takes time and effort, as almost everything worthwhile seems to do. And it may require an outlay of maintenance money. But remember that you have a large investment to protect. You want your car to be working well while you need it, and you want it to be worth as much as possible when you are ready to sell it or trade it in.

So start right out with maintenance as soon as you get your car.

Dealership Maintenance

Use the manual or handbook that came with your car to determine when to take it back to the dealership for regular checkups, safety inspections, lubrication, and nut tightening.

You don't have to be absolutely precise in your timing, but try to stay close to the recommended schedule. A delay of a month or 500 miles might make a lot of difference in a new car's performance.

Look at the checkup almost as if it were a physician's examination. Don't put off your visit because you can't find a convenient time to be without a car. Inquire about a loaner, either as a no-cost courtesy or a low-cost rental, if you really *do* need a car for that day or two.

The best of dealerships cannot go out and find the cars that need to be serviced. In general it is the customer's responsibility to remember to get his car to the dealership for the professional servicing that is due it.

After the warranty period has expired, the owner can take a great number of maintenance measures. Not only can you save a great

I'll fix it myself, if it's the last thing I do!

deal of money in the long run, since mechanics command an increasingly large hourly labor charge per job, but you can gain real satisfaction from doing such things when they need to be done.

People who want to learn how to do simple and basic adjustments, repairs, and replacements can find out directly from knowledgeable friends, from illustrated books and pamphlets on fixing autos, or by watching a mechanic at work. You could also consider taking a hands-on auto repair course at a community college.

But if you really don't *know how* to do something, don't experiment. It could cost you far more to remedy something done wrong than it would if you had paid for normal servicing to begin with.

Do-It-Yourself Maintenance

Preventive maintenance will help your car last longer and look better. The following procedures are ones that you can do yourself, with a minimum amount of knowledge or equipment.

Always follow your owner's manual for proper servicing to maintain your warranty. Keep written records of the service dates and mileage at time of servicing.

AIR FILTER

Check the air filter attached to the carburetor. If you cannot shine a flashlight through the paper of the filter, or see abundant daylight when holding it up against the sun, it is time to change it. You can buy the filter at an auto supply store for a few dollars and readily replace it yourself, at a considerable savings over what you would pay at a dealer's or a repair garage.

OIL AND OIL FILTER

Many people do not seem to realize that they can easily check the oil level in their engines by using the dipstick, which must be wiped off (to get rid of residual oil from a higher level) and then reinserted. If the oil level is low, simply add a can or so of the proper weight of oil for your car. (A special long-necked funnel can be useful in avoiding oil spill.) This quick procedure can save you many dollars in a year's time, since you can purchase oil at a much cheaper price than you would pay a gas station or service garage to do it for you. True, you might get a bit dirty at times in the process, but the smudges are removable. After doing it a few times, you'll begin to wonder why you never did this before.

The oil and oil filter should be replaced every 3,000 miles—or every two months if you do a lot of stop-and-go driving. If you drive more than 10 miles a day to work or do a lot of highway driving, then every 6,000 miles or six months is sufficient.

Motor oil by itself never wears out and never gets dirty. The "dirtiness" is caused by the stop-and-start driving that is peculiar to city and congested freeway driving in metropolitan areas. Unburned fuel gets into the oil, causing it to break down. If you traveled only on open freeways you could probably drive from coast to coast, turn around twice, and travel 20,000 miles altogether without ever having to change oil or even add more than a couple of quarts. In the same amount of mileage, under city driving conditions, you might have had to change oil six or seven times.

WINDSHIELD WIPERS

If your windows smear, streak, or haze up while the wipers are being used, then the wipers need to be replaced. Wipers will also make a whining or grinding sound that should alert you to the need for change.

All you need is to know the make, model, and year of your car. . .and five minutes. Replacement instructions are on the refill box and usually no tools are needed. However, if you do suddenly need a new set, a gas station attendant should be able to take care of this for you at a nominal charge. There is no need to make a special trip to a dealer.

BELTS

It is less expensive and more convenient for you to replace the rubber belts that run various vital mechanisms on the car, such as those on the engine-cooling fan, the water and power steering fluid pumps, the alternator, and the air conditioner. This should be done every twenty-four months or 24,000 miles, with the emphasis on time rather than miles. You don't want to put it off until an aged belt breaks on the open highway, far from a repair service.

A loose or slipping belt, perhaps already in its decline, can cause:
• Overheating, if it is on the fan or water pump
• A low battery, if it is on the alternator

- Noisy and jerky steering, if it is on the power steering pump
- Inefficient air conditioning, if it is on the air conditioner compressor

So if a belt squeals, tighten it! Or if a belt is worn or cracked, replace it as soon as you can!

A word to the wise, especially if you have had the car since it was new: You should replace all belts if one is bad, because they were all put on at the same time—so the rest are probably ready to go, too.

Going on vacation? A good tip is to take extra belts along, especially if you drive a foreign car. Otherwise, you may experience long delays in getting faulty belts replaced.

HOSES

Check all the hoses that transport the essential liquids circulating in the car's working mechanisms—water, oil, and power steering and transmission fluids. If they are spongy, swollen, hard, or cracked around the clamps, replace them. And replace any frozen, corroded, or bent clamps. Retighten clamps about one month after installation. As with belts, if you bought the car new and one hose is bad, they should all be replaced.

COOLING SYSTEM THERMOSTAT

The cooling system's thermostat is vital to a good engine's operation, but easily can be overlooked. It should be replaced every two years. Use a new gasket when you replace the thermostat as well as a gasket sealer.

If the heater delivers cool air, check the thermostat.

PCV (POSITIVE CRANKCASE VENTILATION VALVE)

This valve, which is part of the pollution-control system and is attached to the engine, should be replaced occasionally.

BATTERY

Keep the battery hookups clean of corrosion with a wire brush that you use specially for that purpose. WARNING: Be extra careful when doing so; the powdery material is highly acidic and can severly damage your skin or eyes.

WARNING!! Do not smoke when you are handling a battery.

Gases and acids that are combustible could throw acid on your skin and clothing.

Check the cables. Loose cables or corroded hookups could cause intermittent starting failures. And check the fluid level in the battery. Add water when necessary. (NOTE: Many batteries are now sealed, making this chore unnecessary.)

Increasingly, when a battery or starter fails, drivers are accustomed to getting temporary, emergency starts or "jumps" from the battery of another car. It's a good idea to purchase a jump cable from an auto supply shop or even a large drugstore and keep it in the trunk of your car, for your own or someone else's need.

But be sure you follow the instructions explicitly! It is important to link up properly the positive and negative connections between the two batteries. If this is not done, serious damage might be done to the "live" battery or, far worse, to the cable user himself.

PUTTING ANTIFREEZE OR COOLANT IN THE RADIATOR

You can take care of this simple procedure. Nowadays, it is standard to add this all-purpose chemical to the water in the radiator, to temper the extremes of engine freeze-up or radiator boiling caused by cold weather or overheating the engine. The coolant comes in a bottle that can be bought even in supermarkets and large drugstores. Always follow the manufacturer's explicit instructions in mixing it with plain water.

When the engine is cold:
- Coolant level should be 3 inches below the radiator neck with a crossflow radiator.
- Coolant level should be 1 inch below the filter neck with a downflow radiator.

Warm up the engine enough to feel warmth through the hose to the radiator (but not too hot). Draw a sample of the coolant. (Never remove the pressure cap when the engine is hot!) If it is rusty brown in color, has a loss of color or trace of sediment, it is time to change the coolant. Follow the car owner's manual or some other reliable guide to learn how to drain your radiator.

SPARKPLUGS AND TUNE-UP

Plugs last much longer now because of unleaded fuel and a hotter spark. However, replacing them every year or so will promote better engine performance and extend the life of the expensive catalytic converter. Persistent engine roughness may also mean that the sparkplug wires should be replaced.

Dealerships and other after-market stores, particularly auto supply discount stores, sell do-it-yourself tune-up kits that contain instructions and special tools.

You can make up your own tune-up kit at a savings if you shop at a discount auto supply store. Here are the basic tools you will need for a tune-up as well as general car maintenance:

- Sparkplug wrench
- Feeler gauge to set points, if your car has them
- Gauge to gap the sparkplugs
- Timing light
- Tach/dwell meter
- Compression tester
- Sparkplugs
- Contact points and condenser (not needed if the car has electronic ignition)

LUBRICATION

You can lubricate the door hinges, the trunk and hood hinges, and any other moving parts on the car's exterior, such as the door hood and trunk latches. Use a spray can of white grease or other acceptable lubricant.

To lubricate any major working parts could require an inexpensive hand pump and a tube of grease, along with a knowledge of the location of all the lubricating outlets on your car. If you don't know, have a complete "lube" and oil and filter change done by a professional, while you stand by and watch exactly what is done. Many parts nowadays, however, are self-lubricating.

If you have a front-wheel drive car, you should occasionally have a mechanic give a routine inspection to make sure that there is proper lubrication because this can be a very expensive repair if not properly maintained.

WARNING: Never lubricate belts on the car. They will become saturated and slip.

Again, read your owner's manual!

AUTOMATIC TRANSMISSION AND POWER STEERING FLUIDS

You should check the transmission fluid level whenever the car is lubricated. Use the owner's manual to determine how often the fluid and filter should be changed.

To check the fluid, park the car on level ground with the engine warm and idling in neutral. The fluid should be thin and red or maroon. If it looks dark brown, it's time to change it.

Periodically check the level of the power steering fluid, particularly if you hear a whining or grinding sound as you turn the steering wheel sharply. The fluid is easily purchased and easily poured into the receptacle.

STARTER MOTOR

Turn the key on. If the solenoid clicks but the engine doesn't turn over, the brushes could be worn. This could cause intermittent starting failures. The customer should get an exchange starter from a dealership or auto parts supply store.

TIRES AND WHEELS

The air pressure in all four tires (and the spare tire as well) should be checked at least once a month and certainly before a long trip. Proper inflation is stated in the owner's manual. You can get your own pressure-testing gauge at an auto supply store for just a few dollars. It will prove very handy nowadays in the self-serve islands at gas stations.

Check tires when they are cold. Check the tire tread and sidewalls for cuts or cracks. A tire is considered worn out if it has less than 1/16 of an inch of tread depth in any row of grooves.

Periodic wheel realignment, balancing, and tire rotating are necessary for proper tread wear. You may or may not be able to do the latter chore yourself. The other two jobs should be done by pros. But you can be alert to the need for them by studying the wear patterns on your tires.

As a safety measure, check your wheels periodically to see that the nuts are tightly seated on the bolts, particularly after you have had work done on your tires or wheels. Some mechanics or their assistants are notoriously negligent in seeing that they have been properly tightened. They depend on machines, not their own hands, to do the job, and the bolts tend to work themselves loose after a while, causing a tire to wobble or even come off while the car is moving.

BRAKES

Brakes should be inspected at least once a year, and the fluid in the master cylinder should be checked every 5,000 miles. Unless you're a brake expert, leave the job up to the pros. However, keep alert to possible brake problems. And since brakes are a crucial safety device in any car, you do not want to put off having them checked and/or repaired and replaced.

Indications of brake trouble:

- If the car pulls to one side when the brake pedal is pushed down. This can mean worn suspension parts, worn brake linings, or fluid on the linings.
- When brakes chatter. This can mean a drum is out of round, the lining is loose, or a disc is warped.
- A grinding noise when stopping may mean the brake shoes or pads are completely worn through.
- A spongy-feeling brake pedal may indicate that the brakes are low on fluid or that there is air in the lines. If the brake pedal goes almost to the floor, the fluid may be completely gone!
- If the brakes suddenly go completely out on you on a rainy day— especially likely to happen if you are driving through a flooded area—you have water-saturated brake pads and lining. Drive with one foot on the brake and one foot on the accelerator in order to dry them out rapidly and restore their function.

WAXING THE CAR

A clean, shiny car demonstrates your pride in ownership and capacity for administering TLC (tender loving care). It is also likely to last longer and be more valuable at trade-in time. Most cars should be waxed twice a year.

Some tips about waxing cars:

- Cars exposed to salt, air, road salt, dirt roads, or industrial areas that have heavy fumes, as well as those regularly parked outside, should be washed and waxed more frequently.
- After a rain or during a washing, if the water does not "bead" up, the car most likely needs a waxing.

- At an auto supply store you can purchase special substances to assist you in your waxing and finishing chores. Rubbing compound is an abrasive paste used to remove deep stains and scratches or to smooth out a repaint job. Polishing compound is a milder abrasive used for light stains; the polishing portion produces the gloss. Silicone deposits a thin transparent film that deepens the color of the car.

How to Save Gas Money

Disney World's EPCOT Energy Center in Florida shows that Americans are using energy more efficiently. Conservation is already paying off. We used 10 percent less energy in 1980 than we would have if we hadn't started conserving, and learning conservation habits, in the '70s. By the year 2000 we expect to be using one-third less energy than we would have had we not halted our energy-spending spree.

Another EPCOT attraction in the Disney World Transportation Center shows how air flow or aerodynamics around a car reduces fuel consumption. One of the interesting points is that a car uses 65 percent of the fuel burned just in pushing air!

Here are some suggestions to help you cut down on gasoline consumption:

- Plan ahead and do all your errands in one trip.
- Consider car pooling.
- Ride a bus when you can. Or walk. Or bicycle.
- Accelerate and brake smoothly.
- If you can, buy a new car. They are designed to be more fuel-efficient.
- If you do drive an old car, remember it can run more efficiently with tune-ups, clean filters, radial tires, and friction-reducing oil.
- Using high-grade fuel-efficient motor oil can improve fuel economy by 5 percent.
- Closing car windows saves 1 percent.
- Accelerating slowly up to your desired speed saves 5 percent.
- Each additional 100 pounds of weight in your car lowers fuel economy by 5 percent.
- Using air conditioning at 55 mph lowers fuel economy by 2 to 3 percent.

Saving energy means saving money. And therefore the way we use and drive our cars determines both fuel consumption and cost. Perhaps with the money you'll save by reading this book you can drive in your new car to Disney World to see its energy conservation exhibit yourself!

Where Your Car Lives

Each part of the country presents its own unique problems to cars and their drivers. Extremely cold or hot weather, heavy dust or sand, high humidity, salt air or salt in the road, altitude, and terrain all contribute to the reasons manufacturers have not yet been able to come up with the perfect car, adaptable to each and every circumstance.

Cold, wintry weather causes water to condense in the oil and reduce lubrication. The oil should be changed more often in the winter. Automatic transmissions can be strained when drivers try to rock their cars out of the snow. Rear axles are also affected by the rocking. (It could be cheaper just to have your car towed.) And there's always the possibility of finding your radiator cracked if water freezes and expands—a condition less frequent now because of antifreeze. Salt used to melt down snow and ice on the streets can corrode your car, particularly the underside. Therefore, if your winters come with liberal sprinklings of salt, be sure to wash your car frequently, especially underneath.

Hot climates cause other problems. When the mercury climbs above 100 degrees, the incidence of car problems rises. The battery has to use more amps to start the car. Heat evaporates water in the radiator and battery more quickly, requiring frequent checking. Summer road heat is bad for the tires, and they should be checked for abnormal wear. "Vapor lock" sometimes occurs in heat.

High humidity and temperatures strain the air conditioning system. Drain hoses should be checked twice a season. Humidity shortens the lives of tires and belts, and cars need to be washed more often. Humidity can also afflict the car's electrical system.

High altitudes, with their lower oxygen content, often necessitate a special tuning of your car. There are kits available for this purpose. If you are traveling to such an area, temporary adjustments can be made on your carburetor by a mechanic to let in more air for the mix with the gasoline and to reduce fuel consumption.

Some states, like California, have stricter auto emission control laws to decrease air pollution. To meet these standards, the carburetors use a mixture of less gasoline to air. Therefore the carburetors are touchier, making cars harder to start when they are cold.

Always remember that your car isn't specially designed or built to *have* problems! But it is not capable of enduring all the adverse conditions it may be subjected to.

Fix It—or Trade It In?

When periodically evaluating your present car's strengths or shortcomings, you may find that some essential work is needed to bring its performance really up to par. Or some sudden calamity may befall it: either a malfunctioning of the mechanism itself or damage to its exterior. When something has to be done to your car that goes beyond routine maintenance and repair, you face the question of whether to fix the car up or trade it in.

You must weigh what a new or well-functioning used vehicle will cost against what it would cost to get your car properly repaired. This means shopping among dealers' service departments and auto repair garages, if you are concerned about keeping the price down while getting quality work done.

Don't assume anything or be overly trustful. *Always get a written quote before you have any work done.* And tell the mechanics not to spend 5 cents more than that without your approval! Sometimes people get a price estimate only to find out at the time of picking up the car that the bill did not include parts or your car's labor costs.

Also ask the dealership how much the customer labor rate is. The customer labor rate varies from one area of the country to another and even within some cities. It should be less per hour than what you would pay at a regular repair garage. If it isn't, you should weigh the advantages of having the work done at the dealership versus having it done elsewhere—so long as the work does not require special knowledge or access to special manufacturers' parts.

What you are really interested in is the *final* price—assuming that the work to be done will have the same quality attention wherever you take your car. So your questions must be:
• How much will each item cost?
• The cost of labor separately? And parts separately?
• How much will the total cost be?

There are necessarily some exceptions in obtaining this final price quotation. In some labor operations, for instance, no one knows what has to be done to repair or replace an engine, transmission, or rear end. However, a range can be given to you, such as $200 to $500.

Keep in mind that your car still has a certain value for its various working parts and the body itself, if that is in good shape. Some adept mechanics specialize in cannibalizing parts from one defective car and matching them with those of another car, to make a well-working and good-looking composite auto that will interest used car buyers.

If you must abandon hope for your car and start the whole searching and buying process over again, I hope this book helps you bargain from a much safer and stronger position. And—would you believe it now?—you'll probably actually *enjoy* car buying this time!

Success to you!!!

FIFTEEN

What Make of Car— from Where?

Henry Egghead, who taught business economics at the university, dropped in to see his banker, Green Wad. "My car is just getting too old," he said, "so I'm trading it in on a new one."

"So you want financing," Green Wad commented. "Are you buying a domestic or foreign-made car?"

"Oh, I'm sticking with the Sunrise Rider," Henry said.

"You're really pleased with a Japanese car?"

"Sure," said Henry. "Of course, we've been through a lot together." He sat back in the leather chair and reminisced. "Like once I was attending a big meeting in Detroit, and some nut shot rifle bullets through the window when the car was in the parking lot. We figured it was done by some laid-off autoworker who hated the sight of an import car.

"Then, heading home," he continued, "I began thinking I was out in the Wild West. A mean-looking guy pulled alongside me at fifty-five mph and tried to run me off the road. I stopped to eat a bite a while later, and as I walked up to the restaurant, there he was. He shouted, 'People like you with your Sunrise Rider have put me and my relatives and friends out of work.'

"Well," said Henry, "I was afraid to tell him what I really thought.

Which was, 'If all you people ever put in an honest day's work and used quality craftsmanship, and if your company had made a compact car at a sensible price, I'd have bought one of your USA-made products. It's about time you and your unions and top management worked together—the way the Japanese do.' "

"Hmmm," said Green Wad. And he arranged for the loan.

Some months later Henry Egghead was back in the banker's office—at Green Wad's request. For three months he had failed to make his mortgage and car payments.

"I lost my job," Henry explained sadly. "The government grant didn't come through again on my transportation survey. And the university needed it to pay my salary. The American auto industry, I guess, just wasn't putting enough tax money into the federal coffers. But I hear it is beginning to come back strong now, so there's hope for a new grant, maybe in a half year. Do you think I could—"

Green Wad felt uncomfortable. He knew that his visitor was not used to asking for favors, let alone begging for pity. He looked at him across his wide walnut desk. "Mr. Egghead," he said, "I'll give you thirty days to bring your payments up to date. If you don't you'll have to sell both your house *and* that Sunrise Rider you were so eager to buy when I saw you last."

Henry Egghead felt distraught. But there was a slight compensation for his woes: He had found an absorbing area for a new study. Have American car buyers really consistently *told* their own nation's manufacturers the kind of cars they want them to make? Are the manufacturers themselves finally getting their messages? And do people really think of how the decision of buying foreign vs. domestic might affect them personally?

Circumstances in the automotive industry have dramatically changed in the last fifteen years. No longer are American cars setting the standard for commerce, for sturdy engineering, for popular and practical designing.

Increasingly, U.S. automakers are taking a back seat to foreign manufacturers. They aren't happy about it, nor are their workers, particularly those laid off from jobs they thought would be good for a lifetime.

A major decision confronting most American car buyers is whether to buy a domestic or a foreign-made car.

Survivors never experience an end to an economic battle.

Supply and Demand

When World War II ended, most servicemen came home with a lot of dreams. A big one was buying a new car. Cars, however, were not immediately available. Detroit needed time to return to its prewar position as the center of the automobile industry.

For several years the demand for cars was so much greater than the supply that a fast-moving, seemingly limitless market was created. Many profit-greedy dealers loaded their cars and trucks with every conceivable dealer-installed option and sold them at ridiculously high prices. A number of them became millionaires.

Times have changed, and so have dealerships. In 1949 there were about 50,000 domestic auto dealerships. There are approximately 20,700 dealerships today.

A Lost Love Affair?

New car showings of the past were major events across America. People rushed to these unveilings. An aura of mystery was created through the enticing ballyhoo of automotive advertising.

The suspense, the intrigue, the opportunity, at V.I.P. showings, to see a particular car enchanted millions. And to be able to *buy* a new car before anyone else was a terrific status symbol. When others saw your new car, they wanted one too.

Most accessories were optional on models of the 1950s and '60s. Can you imagine paying extra now for sun visors, all mirrors, padded dashboards, turn signals, backup lights, heaters, power steering, power brakes, or automatic transmissions?

The free enterprise system was very much alive. Owning a stunning car with fancy features was an extremely important part of American life. A handsome automobile, once a luxury, became a necessity. With the population moving to more sparsely settled areas, a huge highway system was built. We all became more dependent upon one another, and distance became a measurement of time rather than miles.

How Japanese Cars Got Going

A team of Japanese experts who were observing American industrial expertise explained that one reason their manufacturers were able to get a good share of the American auto market was that Japan, crushed in World War II, had to start from scratch. The Japanese spent $28 billion for steel blast furnaces. The United States, in contrast, spent only $18 billion because its old ones were intact. The Japanese built 10,000 industrial robots, while the Americans made only 3,000.

As their industries started over, the Japanese set up new programs using Western technology. The Japanese also were not hampered by entrenched attitudes toward production techniques, antiquated facilities, or American labor traditions.

The Japanese business culture applied American methods of technology and employee relations—and improved upon them. Listening to and acting upon employee suggestions is only one example. And they adopted American quality-control principles.

The Japanese automakers feel the increase of automobile imports into the United States is not necessarily the cause of the trouble with the American industry. They say the Japanese increased exports because Americans *chose* to buy Japanese cars. They also declare that the management of the American auto industry and its labor unions should try to be more competitive with them, maintaining that increased competition would make both nations' industries stronger.

America Wasn't Ready for Small Cars

George Romney of American Motors was way ahead of his time. Beginning in 1950, American Motors made a small car, the Metropolitan, but America wasn't ready for it. General Motors introduced the Corvair, the Nova, and the Vega. But each car had extensive problems.

Then the oil embargo came along in the early 1970s. Because until now the American public had not shown sufficient enthusiasm for small cars, the manufacturers had not produced them in quantity. So the fuel crisis found the United States with few small cars.

Motorists rushed out to buy small cars that consumed less fuel. These cars were selling for their sticker prices, and sometimes more. Sales of regular-size cars slowed down and big cars didn't sell well at all. But the American buying public has been fickle, for as soon as the gas situation improved, domestic small-car sales dropped, while big-car sales picked up considerably.

How What You Buy May Affect the U.S. Economy

Dozens of industries are tied in with the manufacture of American cars and their component materials and parts. When the auto industry suffers, many support and peripheral businesses suffer too.

Millions of people are involved in the auto industry, including a million at the manufacturing level and a million at the sub-supplier and retail levels. This doesn't include the peripheral jobs, such as highway work, car insurance sales, and recreation. One out of five people in this nation works directly or indirectly in the automotive industry.

Keeping employment up and more taxpayers on the job not only increases civic pride but makes it easier on your pocketbook. It's worth pondering when you are in the process of purchasing a new car.

The Japanese Way

I focus on Japan as our most formidable foe in world trade because Japanese cars make up 80 percent of total auto imports in this country.

When America sends cars to Japan, they are slapped with heavy protective tariffs.

Protective and restrictive import laws also exist in other countries. The European nations that have auto industries have imposed quotas that limit car imports to a set percent of sales, or to the number of their own cars exported to particular countries.

Many Japanese products also are subsidized by their government, and their own citizens are pressed to "Buy Japanese."

How Do We Get Out of This Downspin?

One of the remedies suggested for the ailing American auto industry has been the introduction of "local content" bills in Congress. The various versions of these bills differ, but basically they all boil down to this:

More and more of the components of cars sold in the United States would have to be made in America. Most of the bills would allow a lower percentage at first and graduate up to as high as 90 percent in the next few years.

Many international trade experts discourage such laws, saying such trade measures are unnecessary since the industry seemed to be picking up somewhat in 1983, with 11.9 percent recovery in January alone. General Motors called 21,000 workers back, and American Motors and Ford were following suit on a more limited scale.

As most people know, U.S. automakers made record profits of almost 14 billion dollars in 1984, and '83 and '84 brought back more than the billions of dollars in working capital that had been lost at the beginning of the decade.

The Effect of Our Government on Car-Buying Habits

But foreign automakers have the U.S. market under a state of siege. Of course, the Japanese continue to sell millions of cars. But the Koreans are coming and have their own franchises—Hyundai Motors, Daewoo Motors and Saehan. Pontiac and Chevrolet will also soon market Korean-made cars.

Just as the American automakers tried hard to outrace the Japanese, the Japanese are now finding their own car industry threatened by the technological advances and low wages in a neighboring Asian nation. The new Korean cars forced the Japanese and American automakers to once again offer stripped-down models at lower prices.

Then there is the low-volume Yugo from Yugoslavia. Built by employees being paid 60¢ an hour who live in apartments they rent for $10 a month, the car can sell for $4,000 to $4,500. (But the Yugo, with little accelerating power, is poor on hilly terrain.)

Mazda also will be building cars just outside of Detroit, with a $6 per hour labor cost advantage over the rest of the U.S. automakers. Many people are watching to see how this concept will work right in the lap of the UAW itself.

While foreign automakers were preparing a major assault on the world car market, another fight was brewing within the United States that would eventually affect the efficient performance, and therefore the desirability, of American-made cars.

Because of the hazards of air pollution to public health, the federal government became heavily involved in instituting and monitoring clean-air regulations. Pollution controls were added to cars in 1968 and became more stringent in each successive year. The government finally backed off in 1981, when it became clear that the embattled American auto industry simply could not accommodate the ever-increasing, expensive forced changes.

Pollution controls installed back in the 1968 domestic cars made the gasoline-powered engines run roughly. Customers complained about the performance, and the engines became increasingly more difficult to work on. Safety and antipollution mechanisms, while necessary, also add to the cost of the car.

Does the U.S. Auto Industry Have a Future?

In 1981 and 1982 the news media often reminded us that the American autoworkers' day in the sun was coming to an end. People with twenty to thirty years of service on the job were being threatened with layoffs.

Yet American automakers managed to close 1984 and 1983 in a very profitable position and 1982 with a profit of at least $500 million, after combined losses of $5.5 billion in 1980 and 1981. Previously, the U.S. automakers showed good profit only with a high volume of sales. But recently streamlined factory policies, revised tax laws, a slowdown in building new factories, and concentration on profitable divisions began to change this.

Payroll cuts, factory closings, and the unfortunate indefinite layoffs of almost 270,000 American autoworkers were other measures. The 1980 and 1981 losses wiped out the American automakers' combined working capital, which totaled $13 billion in 1978.

American manufacturers, in responding to a tough economic period, found a way to make profits while producing at low volume, as some of the import manufacturers have done for years. They will probably never manufacture again in the high volume that they once did, because by making the adjustment to stringent conditions and decreasing the supply of new cars, they found they could accelerate the demand—while pushing up their prices too. So in the immediate future at least, we will not see them return to the high volume of yesteryear. Low supply makes high demand. And high demand permits asking for, and getting, higher prices.

By gearing down, however, the industry is actually further threatened with an inability to compete with foreign production in the long haul. By 1990 U.S. automakers will be producing or assembling only one fifth of the world's auto production.

It is possible that only one of the U.S. producers might remain as a world-class automotive manufacturer. Maybe the four remaining manufacturers could merge and become a single industrial giant. And the possibility of cars not being produced at all in the United States is very real.

The domestic manufacturers have all but conceded their inability to compete with the Japanese in the subcompact field, claiming that the Japanese have at least a $1,500 cost advantage—which includes streamlined plants, variable use of employees, and the ability to produce a car with approximately 100 man-hours, compared with the domestics' almost 200 hours, plus an $8 per hour wage advantage.

However, Honda—the Number 3 Japanese exporter to the U.S.—has attempted to transfer the total Japanese concept of manufacturing into a sizable commitment in Marysville, Ohio. You can be sure that all auto-industry-interested eyes are watching Marysville.

The auto industry will not disappear, but by 1985 it might begin practicing total "outsourcing," with almost all of the work performed outside the manufacturers' physical plants and most of the manufacturing labor done outside the United States itself—wherever the lowest-priced quality labor can be found. Final assembly may or may not actually be done in this country.

The United States is becoming a service-oriented instead of manufacturing-oriented nation. New trades will have to be learned by many of today's blue-collar workers.

Right now there is definitely a pent-up auto market. People have to replace cars that are wearing out. Because of the growing price of cars, the business recession, and high interest rates, they have simply delayed buying.

There is new hope for American cars abroad. In some of the Middle Eastern nations, for example, buyers have notably switched from Japanese to American cars because of their intrinsic elegance, style, and status. Generally they judge American cars as stronger, safer, more comfortable, and more elegant.

Because of the strong U.S. dollar, people who live close to the Canadian border have been going to Canada to buy cars for considerably less money than they would have to pay in their own country, saving up to $1,500. And the new car warranty is honored in the U.S. or Mexico.

Eventually, all manufacturers in the world will be in the same position. It will no longer be a matter of foreign versus domestic cars, all will have their "world cars." They are all thinking and planning in terms of building small or smaller cars. They are also trying to put luxury features into so-called economy cars.

A Question to Ponder

The decision is really yours on the question, "Should I buy American?"

I can only say that when you go out looking at cars, you can perhaps give American cars another chance, keeping in mind that:

• In the past few years American cars have done consistently better than most foreign makes in safety tests.

• Some of their prices are comparably better, too.

Figure it this way: You may save a few dollars on a new car if you buy it without giving any regard to which nation's economy you are helping. But by buying American, you are playing a role in America's ongoing economic recovery.

SIXTEEN

Made in the USA

No one will deny that Americans have a romance with their cars. They spend a large chunk of their time looking at, thinking about, riding in, shopping for, buying, selling, fixing, making, washing, bashing, or junking cars. It is appropriate, then, to present brief histories of the major companies—and at the same time to meet some people behind America's great cars, to learn of their accomplishments as well as their ideas for meeting the challenges of the future.

How Our Craze Began

The 1893 World's Columbian Exposition in Chicago had aroused the curiosity of many people, and the newspapers began to carry stories about the "horseless carriages." From France came word of the exploits of Daimler and Benz with their "road wagons." In 1895, New Yorkers saw three Benz "horseless wagons."

In 1896 Henry Ford built his first gasoline-engine-powered motor car in Detroit, Michigan.

The signs of the times were encouraging. The great inventor, Thomas Edison, announced in the newspapers that the horse was doomed. Up in Lansing, R. E. Olds produced the first Oldsmobile. Alexander Winton of Cleveland drove his auto from Cleveland to New York, making what was called a reliability run. William K. Vanderbilt bought a car to race. All over the nation, people began to read and hear about the marvels of this new transportation invention, of the men who were building automobiles, and of these races they were holding at fairgrounds and parks.

The Big Race

Henry Ford went to work on a racer that he hoped would bring him new opportunities to manufacture automobiles. His chance came in 1901. It was announced in Detroit that Alexander Winton would race his world champion car, the Bullet, at the Grosse Pointe racetrack, a few miles from the city. Henry Ford was one of the two men challenging the champion. When the day of the race arrived, stores and shops closed, and a parade of sixty-eight cars moved out to Grosse Pointe. Three cars lined up for the 10-mile race, but only Winton and Ford got away. At the end of 8 miles, Ford was trailing Winton, but then the Bullet began to sputter, and limped to the finish line behind the racer built by Ford. The newspapers the next day reported that Henry Ford was "now in the first rank of American chauffeurs."

Success Not Predestined

Of the nearly one thousand companies that tried to build and sell motor vehicles prior to 1927, fewer than 200 continued in business long enough to offer a commercially suitable vehicle.

Our country's greatest period of industrial development contributed to the growth of many successful manufacturing businesses, from small beginnings, through the efforts and skills of individuals working together in a system of free competitive enterprise.

American Motors Corporation

On March 1, 1902, the first one-cylinder Rambler automobile was sold, during the Chicago Automobile Show. The early car, with a retail price of $750, was built in Kenosha, Wisconsin, by the Thomas

Let me see . . . V.W. in Pennsylvania . . . Honda in Ohio . . . Nissan in Tennessee and Renault in Wisconsin and Mazda in Michigan . . . while others are brewing.

B. Jeffery Company. In 1916 this company became Nash Motors, in 1937 Nash-Kelvinator, and in 1954 American Motors. The French government's automaker, Renault, became the major stockholder of American Motors in the '70s and jointly designed the first French car to be produced in the United States. Appropriately, they named their successful baby the Alliance.

American Motors is a worldwide company. Since 1958 it has expanded its markets, both domestic and overseas; its passenger cars and Jeep vehicles are sold in every state and in more than 140 countries. AMC's administrative headquarters are in American Center, Southfield, Michigan. The research, engineering, styling, and purchasing departments are located in Detroit. Other departments and plants are scattered throughout the Midwest. And AMC cars and Jeep vehicles are produced in twenty-nine countries.

Ford Motor Company

While Henry Ford was not the first person to build an automobile, his system of mass-producing cars (using assembly-line methods) was a milestone in automobile history. His life provides a good introduction to the company he established.

Ford's Early Life

Henry Ford spent his early life on a farm, a few miles from Detroit, near the River Rouge. On each side of the river were the farms of people who had come to the Midwest to get land of their own. Henry's father, William Ford, was one of these early settlers.

When Henry finished school in 1879 at the age of sixteen, he did what thousands of other farmers' sons were doing—he left for the closest city. Detroit, a bustling place with 100,000 people, was a commercial center for the Great Lakes shipping trade. Detroit was also an industrial center, and Henry Ford went to learn a trade at its shops and factories.

Henry's first job, at the Michigan Car Works, lasted only six days, but he soon found another one at the machine shop of James Flowers and Bros., where he learned about engines and about the tools and machines that made parts for other machines. A few months later he left the Flowers' shop to work at the Dry Dock

Engine Company, where he had greater opportunity to learn about steam engines. When his apprenticeship was over, he became Henry Ford the machinist.

Making the Most of a Low Economic Period

Although 1893 was a hard year of panic for many, it proved a good year for Henry. In Chicago that summer he was able to add to his knowledge of gasoline-powered engines and "horseless carriages."

To be nearer his new job at the Edison Illuminating Company, he moved to 58 Bagley Avenue in Detroit. In the backyard of the new home was a brick shed; here Henry set up his tools and continued tinkering with internal combustion engines.

His first experiment was not long in the making. With a piece of gas pipe, an old wheel, some wire, and other scraps of metal assembled on a long board fastened to the kitchen sink in the Ford home, he made his first model gas engine. Although it sputtered and jumped, it worked.

During the years that Ford worked on his homemade engines, other men were also experimenting with gas engines, and they were just as determined as he was to make them operate successfully.

Ford completed his first automobile in 1896.

Organization of the Henry Ford Company

In November 1901 the Henry Ford Company was organized to manufacture automobiles, but the venture was short-lived, and four months later, Ford was working alone again. During the early months of 1903 more investors were found. And in June 1903 the Ford Motor Company was incorporated. The stockholders raised $28,000 to start the new venture. They included A. Y. Malcomson and an employee, James Couzens; John and Horace Dodge, the owners of a machine shop; Albert Strelow, a contractor; John S. Gray, a banker; Vernon E. Fry, a real estate dealer; Charles H. Bennett, an air-rifle manufacturer; C. J. Woodhall, a clerk; Horace H. Rackham and John W. Anderson, lawyers; and Henry Ford.

The new company rented a building on Mack Avenue in Detroit for $75 a month and prepared to manufacture its automobiles. The new factory was 250 feet long by 50 feet wide. This was adequate space, since the new company did not attempt to make any of the parts for its cars. The Dodge brothers, who owned a large machine shop, made the Ford chassis, a carriage company built the body, and the wheels were purchased in Lansing. Once the parts were brought together, a dozen men assembled, adjusted, and tested the completed car—the early Model A Ford. Soon the car, which sold for $950 in Detroit, was advertised as the "boss of the road." Its two cylinders gave it a maximum speed of 30 miles per hour.

Successful on His Third Try

Although Henry Ford's first two ventures into automobile manufacturing had not been successful, this third attempt showed great promise. By the end of the first year, the Ford Motor Company had sold over 1,700 cars.

By 1906, changes were also made in the ownership of the plant. Some of the stockholders sold out and Henry Ford became the major owner of the Ford Motor Company.

Initially he built automobiles for the wealthy, but soon changed to the belief that every man, no matter what his income, should be able to own an automobile. The Model T was built with this in mind. This car, which first appeared in October 1908, brought financial success to Ford and his company. Besides the low price, the engine was "get-at-able," an important feature at a time when most automobile owners repaired their own cars. By the end of 1908, more than 300 Model T's had been shipped to dealers throughout the nation.

Ford's "secret" of success was: have a simple design, use the latest machinery, standardize the parts, make the entire automobile yourself, and always have a good supply of materials on hand. Throughout the rest of his life, he held to these principles.

By 1911 Ford cars were manufactured by the hundreds of thousands. The process of assembling automobiles received more and more attention, and by 1914 a Ford car could be put together in an hour and a half. By the end of 1915, a million Model T's had been produced, and in the next eleven years, fourteen million more were placed on the market. In 1925 nearly 10,000 Fords were completed in a single day in Ford's plants. The vastly popular Model A first appeared in 1927.

Following his success in 1914, Ford announced that his company would have profit sharing for its employees and that the workday would be cut from nine to eight hours. He also set a minimum wage of $5 a day for every employee over the age of twenty-one.

Nineteen seventy-eight was a peak sales year for Ford. It sold 6,557,302 cars, trucks, and tractors worldwide with net sales of $42.8 billion.

In 1984 Ford sold 5,667,162 cars, trucks, and tractors worldwide with net sales of $52.4 billion, and profits of $2.9 billion.

Ford Motor Company maintains manufacturing, assembly, or sales facilities in twenty-nine countries and does business on six continents.

General Motors Company

The founding of General Motors on September 16, 1908, drew little attention. Motorcar firms were appearing virtually everywhere. But since that day, G.M. has become one of the most widely known of industrial organizations.

The nucleus of General Motors was the Buick Motor Car Company. It was formed in 1902 by David Buick in Detroit and later moved to Flint, Michigan, where it was managed by William Crapo Durant of the Durant-Dort Carriage Company. At the time that the General Motors Company was being incorporated as a New Jersey firm, Flint had a population of about 25,000 and four streetcars.

Early or charter members of the infant G.M. cluster were Buick, Oldsmobile, Cadillac, Oakland (now Pontiac), Ewing, Marquette, Welch, Scripps-Booth, Sheridan, and Elmore, together with Rapid and Reliance trucks. The other automotive division, Chevrolet, joined the group in 1918.

By the end of 1909, Durant had gathered twenty-two concerns and plants into General Motors, by purchase of all or part of their stock. Only four of the car lines—Buick, Oldsmobile, Cadillac, and Oakland—continued making cars for more than a short time after their purchase by G.M.

By 1911 the idea of a general staff organization had gained acceptance in the company. A testing laboratory also was established—as the annual report said, to "serve as an additional protection against costly factory mistakes and give the purchaser. . .an additional guarantee not merely for his comfort, but to assure his safety."

Kettering Self-Starter Increases G.M. Leadership

As G.M.'s organization was taking shape in Michigan, an engineering event that was to have much to do with G.M.'s subsequent leadership in research was occurring in Dayton, Ohio—the introduction of the electric self-starter designed by Charles F. "Boss" Kettering, the automotive research pioneer.

Designed by Kettering at his Dayton Engineering Laboratories Company, the electric self-starter first appeared in 1912 Cadillacs and, by doing away with the dangerous and unpredictable hand crank, popularized motoring. More than any other single development, this electric self-starter was credited with making motorcars more usable, by women drivers especially.

Boss Kettering became the scientific mastermind of the G.M. Corporation, in charge of its unparalleled research and engineering programs. He joined G.M. in 1920 when the Dayton Research Laboratories were merged into G.M. and moved the Research Laboratories to Detroit in 1925. He remained with the corporation until his retirement on June 2, 1947.

General Motors Corporation Founded

The General Motors Company officially became General Motors Corporation on October 13, 1916, when incorporation papers were filed in Delaware. By August 1, 1917, the new corporation had acquired all of the stock of General Motors of New Jersey, which was formally dissolved two days later.

At about that time, Alfred P. Sloan, Jr., who as both president and chairman gave G.M. its present managerial philosophy and who was to guide General Motors from 1923 until 1956, became associated with Durant. Sloan had built up a $50,000 investment in the Hyatt Roller Bearing Company of Harrison, N.J., to assets of about $3.5 million in twenty-four years. Hyatt was brought into G.M. through the United Motors Corporation for $13.5 million.

In 1916, the new G.M. Corporation sold 25,000 cars and trucks for 19 percent of U.S. car and truck sales in its first full year. Net sales totaled $29,030,000 and its payroll at the peak numbered more than 14,000, mostly in Michigan. At the end of 1920, in the midst of a nationwide economic crisis, G.M. was on the verge of financial collapse. In 1921 it had only 12 percent of automobile sales.

By contrast, in 1979 G.M. sold 8,993,000 cars and trucks worldwide with net sales of $66.3 billion and employed an average 853,000 workers. In 1981 G.M. sold 6,800,000 cars and trucks worldwide, with net sales of $62.7 billion and employment averaging 741,000 workers. In 1982 G.M. sold 6,244,000 cars and trucks with net sales of $60 billion. G.M.'s '84 and '83 net sales of $83.9 billion and $74.6 billion netted profits of $4.5 billion and $3.7 billion.

The 1920 crisis marked the turning point in General Motors' history. A new leadership took over. A new concept of management was forged, and a new approach to product and production emerged. Coordinated policy control replaced the undirected efforts of previous years.

Durant resigned the presidency on November 20, 1920, to be succeeded by Pierre S. DuPont, who elevated Sloan to become his first assistant executive vice president. An entirely new management policy was begun and on May 10, 1923, Sloan succeeded to the presidency.

Growth under Sloan's Leadership

This new management concept has been acknowledged as a milestone in business administration, with Sloan, its principal architect, considered a pioneer of modern management.

Fundamentally, it involves coordination of the enterprise under top management, direction of policy through top-level committees, and delegation of operating responsibility throughout the organization. Within this framework, management staffs conduct analysis, advise policy committees, and coordinate administration.

Under Sloan, General Motors began its period of greatest growth. The auto firm that in 1923 accounted for about 20 percent of new car sales in this country went on to become the largest producer of cars and trucks in the world.

An Organization of Organizations

General Motors strove to maintain a balance between individual and group management, with Sloan working to establish a good management structure.

At the corporate level, Sloan's idea was to establish "decentralized operations and responsibilities with coordinated control." At the individual level, his policy was simple: "Give a man a clear-cut job and let him do it."

G.M. in 1984 had 151 facilities in 90 cities in twenty-six states in the United States. In addition, G.M. of Canada operated thirteen plants and G.M. had assembly, manufacturing, distribution, sales, or warehousing operations in thirty-seven other countries. Subject to broad overall policies and coordinated control of the central organization, the thirty operating divisions and subsidiaries served the United States and Canada.

General Motors still follows the organizational philosophy of the brilliant Alfred P. Sloan, the man who led G.M. out of near bankruptcy in the 1920s. General Motors has been "downsizing" cars since 1977.

G.M. is currently building a new franchise dealer network with an all-new car, the Saturn, in an all-new corporation. It is a joint venture with the UAW and G.M. employees. The Saturn will debut as a 1989 model. Lloyd Reuss and William Hoglund are in charge of this project and the success or failure of Saturn will determine the future of the manufacturing of cars on this continent. Chrysler is also planning a high-technology car and claims it will beat G.M. to the marketplace.

We may eventually see fewer car lines at G.M.—perhaps only a big car line and a small one. Also there will be firmer distinctions between prices and car lines—in other words, definite makes representing low, medium, and high. Also, we will see more multiline dealerships. G.M. has made it more favorable to be an investor in an automobile dealership, now that dealers are allowed to own more than one G.M. dealership and remain involved indefinitely.

Roger Smith of General Motors became the auto world's reigning financial genius in 1984 thanks to the enormous profits and many other accomplishments of his leadership as chairman of the corporation. If his latest innovations succeed, he and Jim McDonald, president, could take a place in automaking history next to Alfred Sloan and William Durant.

Chrysler Corporation

Chrysler Corporation was founded on June 6, 1925, through the energy, imagination, and determination of Walter P. Chrysler. He dreamed of an "engineered car" that would be safe, attractive, and comfortable, and could be sold at a moderate price.

By the time he was eighteen, Chrysler had built a miniature steam locomotive, 28 inches long and complete in every detail, including air brakes and a tiny whistle that blew—and it ran too. In 1895 he became a journeyman machinist, and at the age of 33 Chrysler became superintendent of locomotive power for Chicago Great Western Railroad—the youngest man ever to hold a position of such importance.

In this same year, 1908, Chrysler bought his first automobile. At the Chicago Automobile Show that year, he purchased a Locomobile for $5,000, borrowing $4,300 to add to his own $700 savings. Chrysler did not buy this car to operate it. He bought it to study, take apart, and reassemble several times. Sixteen years would pass before Chrysler built the first car to bear his name. Meanwhile, he joined the American Locomotive Company. In 1912 he became works manager of the Buick Motor Company. Within five years he was its president and general manager. And in 1919 Chrysler also became first vice president of General Motors in charge of manufacturing.

Having become a millionaire at forty-five, Chrysler retired—but not for long. In 1920 he went to work for Willys-Overland and soon after Chrysler sought to revitalize the Maxwell Motor Car Company, possessor of 90% ownership of Chalmers Motor Corporation.

While putting new life into the sagging company, Chrysler thought about his dream car, one with a high-compression engine. And he acquired an engineering staff that designed and successfully tested America's first medium-priced and high-styled automobile—the Chrysler Six. This new car was displayed in January 1924. That year almost 32,000 Chryslers were built and sold by Maxwell dealers— then a record for first-year car sales.

By the fall of 1925, nearly 3,800 dealers were selling Chrysler cars. By 1926 the new corporation had forged from twenty-seventh to fifth place in the industry. By 1927 the firm was fourth in new car sales with 192,000 units.

The year 1928 was the most momentous in the early history of Chrysler Corporation because then Chrysler launched two new cars—the Plymouth and the DeSoto—and purchased the Dodge Company, one of the industry's largest companies.

By 1929 Chrysler Corporation had arrived as one of the Big Three automobile companies. And a few years later, the sales of the six-cylinder 1933 Plymouth outstripped its manufacture. Before the year's end, output rose from 1,000 to 1,200 cars a day.

In spite of the Great Depression, Chrysler strengthened its place in the industry in the '30s and gained a reputation for being tough and competitive. In 1933 it was the only automotive firm to surpass its sales record of the 1929 boom year.

Today there are some thirty-seven Chrysler Company manufacturing plants in the United States, Canada, and Mexico. Chrysler was threatened with bankruptcy in 1980. But the federal government bailed it out, and the company is getting back on its feet under the guidance of Lee Iacocca, its chairman of the board.

Lee Iacocca and his people resurrected Chrysler. They did so well that they even prepaid the government-guaranteed loans. Lee, who was personally rewarded with millions of dollars in income, became the Cinderella of the auto industry and the darling of many Americans who admired his entrepreneurial spirit. However, he is no longer as actively involved on a day-to-day basis as he once was. Gerald Greenwald, Harold Sperlich, and Bennett Bidwell are at the helm, while Lee fills the role of the PR man he is and always has been.

The Power of the Automakers

Most businesses operate with good or bad seasons, months, or years. In the car business the gauge is a day, every day. This creates a unique pressure on the car dealer. Car dealers are expected to make things happen.

So I must close with one of the many success stories about the franchised dealers, the movers and shakers, who make things happen for the automakers.

THE TALE OF GLENN AND MUREL HUMPHREY

Glenn and Murel Humphrey were both born in Laurens, Iowa. Their father was a livestock speculator who moved his family to South St. Paul, Minnesota, where the brothers went to high school. Glenn graduated from high school with knee patches but he knew it would not always be that way. His first job was with a Ford dealer in St. Paul, and when A. C. Hall moved to Milwaukee in 1926 to take over a Chevrolet dealership, Glenn moved along, remaining with Hall for nine years.

Glenn Humphrey eventually bought Avenue Chevrolet and on July 20, 1936, he opened the doors of Humphrey Chevrolet in Milwaukee.

Murel joined his brother in 1941, rejoining him again in 1946 after the war. They worked well together and one of the reasons for their success was their tireless attention to detail. They were not mechanically inclined, but they knew how to sell and operate. As the business grew to twenty-two corporations, they had car dealerships representing all of the G.M. car divisions, along with a finance company, insurance company, leasing company, and a real estate company. They became one of the top ten car dealers in the United States.

To their managers, they were known as "Thunder" and "Lightning." Glenn was Thunder due to his boundless energy and dynamic and driving ways. Murel was the follow-through man. Their managers presented them with a long whip one Christmas to remind them of their whip-cracking. It hung behind their desks on the fireplace wall. They were in touch with their managers on a daily basis (sometimes even on Sundays).

Both brothers were Masons—Glenn became the Potentate of Tripoli Shrine in Milwaukee and a 33rd Degree Mason. They also took the time to become involved in the community and state, with many awards to show for it.

The Humphreys trained many young men in the auto industry, giving them a chance to become managers of their own dealerships.

Neither took off much time because business came first. . . . They built an empire long to be remembered!

About the Author

Gordon Thomas Page has spent all of his adult working life in the retail automobile business. For more than twenty-six years he has been, successively, a car salesman, sales manager, dealer, and independent consultant.

Gordon grew up, appropriately, in Detroit, Michigan. There at age five he operated a profitable Kool-Aid/lemonade stand. He also cut grass, raked leaves, and shoveled snow. Later on he had two successful *Detroit News* delivery routes. The Kiwanis Club paid for his membership in the Northeastern YMCA because he was a so-called kid from the inner city, the east side of Detroit.

Gordon acquired his long and intensive involvement with the automobile industry naturally, through his father. Ed Page, who called himself a hard-headed hillbilly, came from Greenville, South Carolina. He worked in auto assembly plants for eighteen years, first for the Packard Motor Company and later for the Chrysler Corporation at the Dodge Hamtramck Plant, where he served in Trim Department 99 and also as a millwright. In the 1930s and '40s Ed was a "headbuster" or "goon," as it was called, for the unions. In 1954 he started selling cars for Don McCullagh Chevrolet, billed as "The World's Largest Chevrolet Dealership." When Ed Page died in 1971, he was still selling Chevrolets.

Growing up, Gordon worked as a truck driver, janitor, shoe salesman, short-order cook, construction laborer, mechanical draftsman, and product designer. A graduate of Cass Technical High School, he was a member of Wayne State University's Class of '58. He spent the summer of 1957 in Europe with the college's men's glee club in a USO tour entertaining American troops.

Gordon Page started to work for Don McCullagh Chevrolet in January of 1958. Both his father and general manager Lynn Wertz had tried to talk him out of going into the retail auto business. "This is no business for a clean-cut young man; it will make a bum out of you," was what they implied, if not downright stated. Yet Gordon soon became the top salesman of the dealership. After he accepted the position of truck manager at Dick Shalla Chevrolet, his team doubled the volume the first year. He then went on to become the dealership's sales manager.

In 1968 Gordon Page bought a Chevrolet-Oldsmobile dealership in Athens, Ohio. It had a 585 Planning Potential—meaning that the presale study had indicated a potential of 585 car sales per year. During the first year, Gordon turned a five-figure loser into a six-figure winner. This success was a result of 31 percent penetration of total passenger car sales for Chevrolet, 10.8 percent with Oldsmobile, 46 percent with trucks, and 18 percent increased fixed overhead absorption.

While in Athens, Gordon Page was very active not only in his business but also in the community. He served as both a Chevrolet zone and Chevrolet regional dealer council member in the Midwest region, in Cincinnati. He was president of the Athens Auto Dealers Association, chairman of the Ohio University Trustees' Academy, vice president of the Kootaga Area Council of Boy Scouts, and district chairman of the Hock-Hocking District of the Boy Scouts of America.

In 1977, after nine years in Athens, Page purchased a 2,135 Planning Potential Metro Chevrolet dealership—the former home for Humphrey Chevrolet in Milwaukee, one of General Motors' largest dealerships in the mid-'60s. The showroom, near downtown, displayed sixty cars. The huge complex—six buildings in all—contained over 100,000 square feet of interior space and was spread out over four city blocks.

Gordon Page's stated policy was: "Our obligation begins when we deliver you a new Chevrolet. This license plate makes you a very special Page customer, and is recognized by our personnel. Service satisfaction is what you should get. Service satisfaction is what we aim to give. We lead in total value by putting you first: parts and service, open the hours convenient to customers."

Recently, Gordon T. Page took a hard look at the automotive business, made some difficult decisions, and changed direction. He has become a highly successful independent international consultant to the automotive industry. He operates his advisory service as Gordon/Thomas/Page & Associates, P.O. Box 432, Brookfield, WI 53008-0432.

Index

Notes:

Notes:

Notes:

Notes:

Notes:

Notes:

Notes:

Notes:

Notes:

Notes: